7 1/2 Places of Wonder

7 1/2
Places of Wonder

Munich, Dubai, Florence, Andalusia,
Oxford, Jerusalem, and two Baltic Sea Cities
[St. Petersburg and Stockholm]

Reflections of a Delighted Traveler
by
Rose Marie Curteman

A Tigress Publishing Book

ISBN: 978-1-59404-048-1
LCCN: 2011944842

Library of Congress Control Number: 2012
Printed in the United States of America

10 9 8 7 6 5 4 3 2 1

Interior Layout: Steve Montiglio

All rights reserved. No part of this book may be transmitted in any form or by any means, electronically or mechanically including photocopying, recording or by any information storage or retrieval system without the written permission of the publisher except where permitted by law.

Requests for such permission should be submitted to:

Tigress Publishing
www.tigresspublishing.com
info@tigresspublishing.com

Author's Note: To protect the privacy of others, I have changed all names and some indentifying facts of all non-public figures.

Copyright 2012 Rose Marie Curteman

*This book is dedicated
to
Nicola, Antonio, Alexia, and Raffaele*

Epigraph

"Life is not measured by the number of breaths we take but by the places and moments that take our breath away."

— Annonymous

Introduction	1
Chapter 1 Munich	3
Chapter 2 Dubai	25
Chapter 3 Florence	53
Chapter 4 Andalusia	85
Chapter 5 Oxford	111
Chapter 6 Jerusalem	135
Chapter 7 Two Baltic Cities	165
i) St. Petersburg	167
ii) Stockholm	185
Afterword	197
Acknowledgments	
Author Bio	

Introduction

"The nectar of life is sweet only when shared with others."
—Adam Mickiewicz

My "places of wonder" are more than the sum of their natural qualities, although each has been generously endowed with pleasures for the eye.

Beyond the physical, they possess a spiritual dimension, a courageous aspect, which to my mind has been too-little touted in other travel writings. I'm drawn to locales that are beautiful, of course, but I also want to know about the people who lived there, how they led their lives, met their challenges and survived, often against great odds. While I rejoice in the world's natural wonders, I rejoice even more in those magical moments when the human spirit breaks free—when its energy ignites, often vaulting to new stellar heights.

Some of these places of wonder have produced individuals who have shaped world events, and excelled in science, literature and other arts; some have been fraught with wars and destruction but held their own. A few have spawned great centers of learning—one, a long-ago Silk Road stop, became a desert fantasy; two have fought political oppression; one is said to be the threshold to heaven. To my way of thinking, all these places of wonder hearten and uplift, reminding us of what is possible.

Sages tell us that all journeys are spiritual, because all

1

demand an element of faith. All impose risk, yet have the potential of opening our hearts and minds, of showing us parts of ourselves that might otherwise lie dormant.

Simply put, travel instructs. It can reduce prejudice, instill humor and reinvigorate body and soul. A case in point: I spent several years living in the vicinity of Bedouins, an experience I describe more fully in my Dubai chapter. Each time I stepped away from their world and back into my own, I was struck by our remarkable commonality—and in time their greatness. Granted, externals were different, but on a deeper level, Bedouins came across as virtuosos of the art of living: I grew to revel in their sense of hospitality, generosity, and capacity for friendship.

You might ask, why focus on these particular places of wonder? Aren't there thousands of others equally worthy?

Yes, there are, but these wondrous places spring from my own life experience: I have lived or spent meaningful time in each of them.

As these pages came together, the first question I was usually asked centered on the "½" in the title. Most of my encounters with these wondrous places were of some duration—in some cases, years. In comparison, I had a relatively fleeting exposure to the two Baltic Sea cities that together contribute to the "½" in my book's title. I include them because my abbreviated encounters in St. Petersburg and Stockholm were so unexpectedly rich and, at times so moving that I intend to return very soon and wish to encourage you to visit them as well.

In the meantime, I bask in what has come my way and happily share the pleasure.

1
Munich

(München)

> *"[Munich is] a German dream translated into life."*
> —Thomas Wolfe

Andreas and I were sipping cappuccinos in an open-air *Kaffeehaus* on Munich's poplar-lined Leopoldstrasse.

I pointed across the street to a billboard which proclaimed, *München ist die Deutsche Stadt mit Herz* (Munich is the German city with heart).

"Can you elaborate on that?" I asked my German friend.

Andreas was pleased that I'd asked, since it gave him an opening to boast of his city's long-standing love affair with art and culture, especially with the antiquities of southern Europe. He told me that for northerners traveling south, Munich offers a first taste of those Mediterranean cultural splendors that have lured Northern Europeans for centuries. "Even our sky here can take on the Mediterranean's translucence," he said, and pointed out that Munich is closer to Venice than to Berlin.

I told him that having lived in Italy, I could understand the city's fascination with the South.

He mused that perhaps this fascination lay with the sunny climate, the relaxed lifestyle, and the diversity of cultures that

Italy affords. "Whatever draws northerners across the Alps to the South," he said, "Munich has long served as a bridge to it."

A cornucopia of the Baroque and the Rococo, Munich offers artistic masterpieces on a par with Italian and French works. After 1816, under the influence of Ludwig I and his brilliant court architect Leo von Klenze, Munich strove to become the "New Athens." Its architectural landscape began leaning heavily toward the Neo-Classical style, a look reminiscent of ancient Greece and the Italian Renaissance. We can feast on such celebrated structures as the Ludwigstrasse, the Alte Pinakothek,* both in the Italian Renaissance style; and the Glyptothek, a stunning Neo-Classical building, housing Ludwig I's Greek and Roman sculptures.

Answering my question about the billboard, Andreas said, "In the end, Munich is about beauty, which we all know can stir the heart and spark the imagination."

He cited a building that is emblematic of this city's passion for beauty: the Residenz, for five hundred years the seat of Bavarian rulers.

It was redesigned in Ludwig's reign by von Klenze in the Italian Renaissance manner, noted for its square, symmetrical architecture. Andreas seemed to agree with those who say the Residenz is reminiscent of the Pitti Palace in Florence.

Its famous bejeweled Cuvilliés Theater, consisting of just five hundred seats, may be Europe's premier surviving Rococo theater. Renovated from 2004-2008, it reopened on June 14, 2008, with a new production of Mozart's *Idomeneo*. Andreas was in attendance.

---

*The Alte Pinakothek, one of the world's leading art galleries, is situated in the Kunstareal, an art-abundant area that further consists of the Königsplatz, Glyptothek, Staatliche Antikensammlung, Lenbachhaus, Neue Pinakothek, Pinakothek der Moderne, Museum Brandhort, and the Staatliche Sammlung für Ägyptische Kunst.

Andreas and I had both been born in wartime Germany—
he in Heidelberg and I in Munich. When I was a baby, my family
moved to Würzburg, a town in northern Bavaria famous for its
university (where Roentgen discovered X-rays), to live out the
war years. In my first book, *My Renaissance: A Widow's Healing
Pilgrimage to Tuscany*, I discuss how on March 16, 1945, the
Allies carried out a devastating nighttime aerial attack that left
Würzburg eighty percent destroyed. Miraculously, not a single
member of my extended family was killed; we were, however,
left homeless with only the clothes on our backs. I also describe
how a mysterious gypsy evacuated us to a village about thirty-
five kilometers away. It was here that I attended the first grade
of school. Eventually, my family and I relocated to Heidelberg,
where Andreas and I met in a high school history class.

I remember Andreas as a straight-A student, sitting at a
desk in front of mine, studious and shy. His legal career has
since whipped the shyness out of him. While Andreas studied
law and dabbled in art history in Munich, I attended college
in the United States—supposedly for a semester or two, but
one thing led to another and, in time, I made my life there. In
spite of our divergent paths, we've remained in touch, meeting
occasionally with our respective families. Now we're both
widowed and reconnect when I am in Europe to reminisce—in
German, of course!

But on this bright summer afternoon, we were happy just
to bask in the parade in Munich's liveliest district, Schwabing,
which some say is the nerve-center of the city's creative life. In
1890, Schwabing was officially incorporated into Munich, and
soon took on the aura of Paris and Montmartre. It typified a
break with Germany's rigid past, attracting writers, poets, actors,
painters, and intellectuals such as Thomas Mann, Hermann
Hesse, Rainer Maria Rilke, Paul Klee, and Wassily Kandinsky.

Even today, Schwabing is considered less a place than a state of mind. Near the university, full of cafés, pizzerias, art galleries, cinemas and discos, it now attracts Munich's smart-set, the *schickeria* or *schickimickis*. I noticed that when the *schickeria* meet, they don't just offer the famous German (bone-cracking) handshake. Instead, they give each other *bussis* (kisses) on both cheeks. They say an energetic *tschau* instead of the more melodious Italian *ciao, tschüss* instead of *Auf Wiedersehen*. They are young, stylish, and golden.

As we watched the "Schwabing hip" pass before us, Andreas commented that these days only the smart-set can afford the district's astronomical rents. "Schwabing has become Munich's most coveted place to live," he said. Struggling artists have long ago retreated to cheaper districts—like Haidhausen. Others have moved to outlying farm houses that are more affordable. These days, up and coming artists consider still another Munich district—Bogenhausen—to be the "in" place in which to live.

Schwabing is many things, among them, the place where I took my first breath. I'm curious about Munich and return here often. The city buoys my spirit, electrifies my heart, and gives me a feeling of rootedness.

As our waiter strolled by, Andreas ordered us some wine, aiding my retreat even further into the mood of the moment.

Munich was first occupied around A.D. 750 by Benedictine monks, or *Mönche,* from whom it took its name München. During World War II, seventy-one allied bombing raids destroyed eighty percent of the city, leaving about 6,500 residents dead and three hundred thousand homeless. The raids also created an estimated five million cubic feet of rubble that took two years to clear. Fortunately, city fathers had the foresight to move most of Munich's art treasures into safekeeping.

It was in Munich that Hitler made his initial power grab in 1923, and here also where the terrorist attack on Israeli athletes occurred during the Summer Olympics of 1972. As Andreas said once, "Dark times have a way of instructing. They teach humility and resilience."

Today, following a meteoric recovery, Munich's population hovers around one-and-a-half million, making it Germany's third largest city, after Berlin and Hamburg. Along with being a cultural enclave, Munich is also the capital of the German Federal State of Bavaria, staunchly Catholic and commanding great autonomy within Germany's federal system.

It is now even a burgeoning business center. Global players such as Siemens and BMW have long been Munich-based, but in recent years biotechnology, software and other service industries have made impressive economic inroads. Only New York City publishes more books. Munich is Germany's film-making capital and the Oktoberfest's playground.

After our wine arrived and we toasted our time together, Andreas insisted on telling me a joke: "In heaven the cooks are French, the police are British, the mechanics are German, the lovers are Italian, and everything is organized by the Swiss. In hell the cooks are British, the police are German, the mechanics are French, the lovers are Swiss, and everything is organized by the Italians."

I chuckled, though I couldn't help but defend my Italian friends. "Actually," I said, "I find the Italians more charming than disorganized."

Andreas smiled and said in his melodic Bavarian accent, "*Es war ja nur ein kleiner Witz*" (It was just a little joke).

With the afternoon still young, Andreas and I walked along Schwabing's great boulevard, Leopoldstrasse, past the Siegestor (Victory Gate) that marks Munich's official boundary. From this point forward Leopoldstrasse becomes Ludwigstrasse. I wanted to visit a small square near the entrance of the Ludwig-Maximilian University called *Geschwister-Scholl-Platz,* which honors the memory of Hans and Sophie Scholl, the brother and sister resistance team that bravely tried to thwart Hitler's advances.

By 1942, Hans and Sophie Scholl had become so disillusioned with all that Hitler had come to represent, that they founded, along with friends, the "White Rose," a nonviolent resistance organization to fight Nazi oppression. From June 1942 to February 1943, the Scholls and their collaborators actively and successfully distributed anti-Nazi leaflets throughout Germany, but by early 1943, their luck ran out. On February 18, while distributing their anti-Hitler fliers, this time on the Ludwig-Maximilian University campus, they were arrested and executed four days later. The movie *Sophie Scholl: The Final Days,** tells their story.

Andreas and I found the square teeming with students and pilgrims like us. Silence permeated the scene—each person alone with his or her thoughts.

We then made our way to the entrance of the Englischer Garten [the English Garden], an urban park since 1808, east of Leopoldstrasse, abutting Schwabing. It is larger than New York's Central Park. In the distance I caught sight of Germany's majestic Alps, just sixty miles to the south.

Whenever I'm in Munich, I try as often as possible to cross the city via the Englischer Garten, a chestnut-and-beech-tree oasis with sweeping lawns, rivers, lakes, boats, and swans for all to enjoy. The Anglo-American soldier, statesman, inventor, and scientist Sir Benjamin Thompson [1753-1814] inspired it. An advisor to Bavaria's Prince-elector Karl Theodor, he received the title of Reichsgraf von Rumford [Count von Rumford] in 1791. Breaking with the "cultivated formality" of the French, in vogue when the park was laid out [1781-1785], Count Rumford persuaded the Bavarians to implement the "natural

---

*Directed by Marc Rothemund; released in 2005.

look" preferred by the English at the time; hence its name and naturalistic layout.

Watching plucky surfers and canoeists negotiating "the big wave," produced by a manmade break in the icy waters of the Eisbach River next to the Haus der Kunst (Museum of Modern Art), I wondered how they would fare among the ten to thirty foot swells on Hawaii's North Shore.

Another park highlight: the naturists who sunbathe nude in the vicinity of the Schwabinger Bach (Schwabinger Creek). As long as the practice was illegal, it flourished; since authorities sanctioned nude sunbathing in 1982, its popularity has waned. Still, from what I saw that day, nudism in Munich is alive and well.

With this as our backdrop, Andreas and I ended our day in the best *schickeria* fashion, with *bussis* on both cheeks and saying *tschüss*. Andreas then headed for Munich's U-Bahn (subway) and I made my way into the park, toward a path along the Eisbach River, an Isar River side-channel that led to my hotel on Keferstrasse.

Walking along the Eisbach River shoreline in the Englischer Garten, I reflected on Thomas Mann (1875-1955), the German novelist, social critic, essayist, and 1929 Nobel laureate. Which of his writings might he have pondered as he walked here, as surely he must have done? He called Schwabing home from 1891 to 1933, until Nazi oppression forced him and his Jewish wife, Katia Pringsheim, into Swiss exile.

In the 1990s, my Seattle book club found Thomas Mann so engrossing that we read him exclusively for over a year: *Buddenbrooks* (1901), *Death in Venice* (1912), *The Magic Mountain* (1924), and *Joseph and His Brothers* (1933-1943).

As Hitler's influence grew in the 1930s, Mann, by then already an émigré, did not hesitate to speak out with loathing for the "swamp of stupidity and meanness" that was Germany then.

Before leaving his homeland, Thomas Mann assumed he would receive forgiveness for abandoning that Germany of then, and would find acceptance following Nazism.

According to his biographer Donald Prater [*Thomas Mann: A Life*, Oxford University Press, 1995] the Hitler regime slashed away at Mann's sense of statehood: In 1936, his honorary doctorate from Bonn University was annulled; soon thereafter he was stripped of his German citizenship. Czechoslovakia then offered him citizenship, as the U. S. did, later.

In the face of continued Nazi repression in Germany and years of exile in Switzerland, Mann emigrated in 1939 to the United States where he taught for a time at Princeton University.

Initially, his public statements about émigré life conveyed a spirit of brave confidence. Publicly, he explored the concept of homelessness, concluding finally that his true home lay in his writings, in the German language, and its manifestations. Anthony Heilbut in *Thomas Mann: Eros and Literature* [Knopf, 1996] quotes Mann: "Where I am is Germany."

But his early self-assurance soon gave way to doubt. Increasingly he spoke of the anguish of exile and homelessness.

I think that Mann's personal experience of exile enabled him to give particular depth to the banished Joseph in *Joseph and His Brothers*, his 1,200+-page retelling of the famous biblical saga, in which Joseph's brothers sell him into slavery in Egypt.

In 1942, Mann relocated from Princeton to sun-swept southern California where, in 1944, he became a U.S. citizen. Yet his longing for home and his mother tongue never left him. In 1952, he returned to German-speaking Switzerland where he died of atherosclerosis in 1955. A German press obituary observed: "A throne has been left empty."

At my hotel was a message from my sister Petra: we would meet for supper at a Biergarten near the Englischer Garten. Her husband, Walter, had been delayed on a business trip to Salzburg and would have to join us on another occasion.

I arrived before Petra and selected a table in the shade of a towering old chestnut tree. A dirndl-clad waitress took my order.

The *Biergarten* phenomenon came into being in the sixteenth century when the threat of fire prohibited the brewing of beer from May to October. Since the demand for beer peaks in the summer, entrepreneurial brewers began producing beer long before the May ban took effect, storing it in cool underground cellars. To promote cooling, they planted shade-producing chestnut trees atop the cellars. And to augment their profits, they eliminated middlemen, selling beer directly to the public. To make the beer-drinking experience more inviting, brewers provided their consumers with tables and benches— anything to prolong their revels. Today more than eighty such establishments thrive in Munich alone.

Petra arrived and once again I was struck by her appearance. She's a decade younger than I, tall, blond, and gorgeous. She stays trim by careful eating and recreational tap-dancing. By training she's a chemist, but she works as the CEO of a small Munich biotechnology company.

After our *bussis* and initial small-talk, we studied the menu. We were tempted to order one of Munich's calorie-laden specialties: *Schweinebraten* (pork roast) or *Leberkase mit Spiegelei* (sautéd meatloaf with egg sunny-side-up). Given Munich's heat, we ordered salads and then shared *ein Kaiserschmarrn* (baked and fried pancake), served with sliced apples and marmalade.

Conversations with Petra glide easily: Family matters come first, especially talk of her husband and their brilliant daughter

Tina, a physician. Then, because of Petra's professional life, our conversation always gravitates to the business arena. My own inclination when in Bavaria's capital is to focus on the city's cultural past, but to my gain, Petra doesn't let that happen.

She explained that her firm is one of some twenty thousand Munich high-tech companies, which now employ a quarter of a million people, and that Munich has Germany's lowest unemployment rate. In fact, Munich ranks fourth in the world for its number of high-tech businesses, after Silicon Valley, Boston, and Tel Aviv.

As to why so many businesses are drawn to Munich, Petra said that one big plus is that the area offers an exceptional quality of life. People like to live where they can enjoy history, culture, the Alps, and even Italy at their doorstep. Companies enjoy a vibrant talent pool. The city has twelve institutions of higher learning with around a hundred thousand students—a source of further potential brain power. The political climate is business-friendly; venture capital is ample.

Of course Germany has a long history of technical and scientific excellence, but this was interrupted by the Nazis. Petra grew pensive when she spoke of the enormous brain-drain brought about by the National Socialists, who drove countless world-class scientists into exile. "In my opinion," she said, "we've still not recovered from those losses. From 1933 to 1990 the United States won 136 Nobel Prizes; Germany a mere twenty-two."

As dusk fell we said good-night. Petra had an early- morning appointment in Augsburg, a city about an hour northwest of Munich. We would meet again before I left Germany.

❁

On the next day, en route to Munich's Marienplatz [St. Mary's Square] in the *Altstadt* [old town], where Andreas and I agreed to meet for our walking tour, I stopped for a cup of coffee at Konditorei Kaffee Hag. Munich now explodes with Starbucks, but Kaffee Hag, founded in 1825, is a city landmark, one I try never to miss. Once the confectioners to Bavarian royalty, the bakery-café remains at its original site, across the street from the Residenz.

As I sipped my coffee and gazed across at the one-time home of Bavarian monarchs, I recalled that a single dynasty, the Royal House of Wittelsbach, ruled Bavaria for nearly eight hundred years, from 1180 to 1918. Descendents of the Wittelsbach family now make their home in a wing of Schloss Nymphenburg, on the outskirts of town.

One of the most colorful (some say eccentric) of the Wittelsbachs was Ludwig II, King of Bavaria (1845-1886). He is also known as the Swan King in English and *der Märchenkönig* (the Fairytale King) in German. Among his accomplishments: Visitors tend to remember him primarily for having built a series of fantasy castles of which Neuschwanstein is the most acclaimed (Neuschwanstein, some say, inspired Walt Disney's creation of the Sleeping Beauty Castle and later the castles in his two famous theme parks), and as the patron of the composer Richard Wagner. However, Bavarians like to remind tourists that Ludwig is also remembered for avoiding wars and funding the construction of the fantasy castles out of his personal income. At that time, these projects created jobs; today their entry fees fill state coffers.

While Germany is today a semi-classless, constitutional democracy, Germans honor their old aristocracy, which was less sullied by Nazism than were the professional classes. Most German aristocrats served unobtrusively in Hitler's armed forces; a few, however, displayed extraordinary daring in their resistance to the Third Reich: The July 20, 1944 failed plot to kill Hitler was largely spearheaded by aristocrats, with German army officer Colonel Count Claus von Stauffenberg (1907-1944) leading the way. He and other ringleaders were promptly captured and shot by firing squad before 1 a.m., July 21, 1944. Stauffenberg's last words were: "*Es lebe unser heiliges Deutschland!*" ["Long live our sacred Germany."] Soon after his death, the Gestapo arrested and imprisoned his widow, Nina Schenk Gräfin von Stauffenberg, then three months' pregnant with their fifth child. The four children were stripped of their names and placed in orphanages. The fifth child, Konstanze, was born in custody in January 1945. After the war, the widow was reunited with her five children and lived out her days near Bamberg, Bavaria. In 2008, the child born in prison, now Konstanze von Schulthess, published in Germany a bestselling book about her mother, titled *Nina Schenk Gräfin von Stauffenberg: Ein Porträt.* In the 2009 movie *Valkyrie*, Tom Cruise depicts von Stauffenberg and his attempt on Hitler's life.

The royal Wittelsbachs, too, did their part to resist Nazi oppression. One operated an anti-Nazi newspaper in Munich; others, for various "misdeeds," landed in Nazi concentration camps.

For their bravery during World War II and overall record of good works, German aristocrats generally [and in Bavaria the Wittelsbachs, specifically] are honored in today's society. The heir to the Wittelsbach dynasty is seen as Bavaria's unofficial head of state. Foreign consuls, for example, call on him to pay their respects. He is addressed as "your Royal Highness."

Lesser aristocrats have assimilated well into German business and other lines of work, living affluent middle-class lives. Some still use their titles; others have dropped them, opting only for the prefix "von." Germans like having their old bluebloods around. They represent a link with tradition and an ethos of doing good. That they offer a little stardust doesn't hurt either.

When I arrived at the Marienplatz, I found Andreas leaning against the square's Fischbrunnen [Fish Fountain], a favorite

Munich meeting-place. His shock of white hair makes him stand out in a crowd. After exchanging *bussis,* I asked him if he'd ever practiced the six hundred-year-old Ash Wednesday superstition of washing one's wallet (or purse) in the Fischbrunnen, to ensure ample money for the rest of the year.

He laughed. "No, but I know people who do and swear by it."

We lingered on the pedestrianized Marienplatz taking in the elaborate facade of the neo-Gothic *Neues Rathaus* (New Town Hall) with its forty-three bells and a three-leveled Glockenspiel with carved dancing figures that perform in summer at 11 a.m., noon, and 5 p.m. The figures act out two episodes from Munich's history: the 1568 wedding of Renata von Lothringen and Wilhelm V, founder of the Hofbräu brewery, and the famous *Schäfflertanz* (dance of the coopers or barrel-makers) which took place at the end of Munich's bout with the plague in 1517.

I especially enjoy watching the eighteen figures, including two jousting knights on horseback, dance around Wilhelm and his bride. At first the knights pass each other, but when they circle around again, the Wittelsbacher (Bavarian), with white and blue colors, defeats the Habsburger (Austrian), with red and white colors, by knocking him backwards.

Andreas said that some criticize this hugely successful tourist attraction as being unduly childlike, but others observe that we all need to be children once in a while.

I've long been interested in the darkened frontage of the Neues Rathaus. "This building seems to have stepped right out of the tales of the Brothers Grimm," I commented, still caught up in its elaborate statuary of assorted festooned nobility, saints, and folk characters from Munich's past.

"Believe it or not," Andreas said, "it's within these fairytale walls that the serious business of Munich's government takes place." I knew that in medieval times the Marienplatz served as the city's salt and corn market. It gained its current name in 1854 when the townspeople appealed to the Virgin Mary to protect them from a cholera epidemic. Each Advent this site becomes Munich's acclaimed *Christkindlmarkt* (Christmas Market), where garlanded stalls sell such wares as handcrafted ornaments, crèche figures, candles, wooden-carved toys, and *Weihnachtspyramiden* (Christmas pyramids).

During one of my December visits years ago I bought a four-tiered candle pyramid and shipped it home to Seattle. Family and friends have delighted in the effect of the candles' rising heat, which activates the device that turns the pyramid, filling the room with a panoply of shifting lights.

Since we were just steps away, Andreas suggested that we stroll over to the Viktualienmarkt, Munich's largest and oldest food market, with a hundred forty stalls, established in 1807. But first I wanted to detour briefly to one of my favorite Munich shopping destinations: Lodenfrey, on Maffeistrasse, a store founded in 1842, specializing in Bavarian costumes along with conventional clothing of excellent quality. Though Andreas was not a shopper, he was a good sport. He even helped me select a red, boiled-wool Giesswein jacket that I expect to last the rest of my life.

The Viktualienmarkt reminds me of a Middle East bazaar. How to negotiate its bounty? Among its offerings: bins of cardamom, cilantro, cumin, saffron, and turmeric; tubs of olives; and more dark purple eggplants than I could count.

In a cooking class I once took, I learned that early eggplant varieties were white-colored; "like large hen eggs," the teacher said. (White eggplants, technically a fruit of East Indian origin, smaller and tougher than the common purple variety, are today considered trendy, although best peeled. The Arabs first introduced this fruit into the Mediterranean area in the 1500s.) My cooking teacher's three favorite eggplant dishes: ratatouille, the

French Provencal stewed-vegetable dish, Turkish musakka, and baba ghanoush, the Middle Eastern dip made of roasted eggplant pureed with tahini, accented with garlic, lemon juice, cumin, salt, mint and parsley. I still prepare all three, using his recipes.

After sauntering in the Viktualienmarkt, we stopped at Fisch-Witte, a bistro that proclaims in English, "If it swims, we have it." Andreas had skipped breakfast and now wanted sustenance. We found a shady nook under an eave. While Andreas savored a cup of bouillabaisse, I enjoyed a cool soft drink.

Then we moseyed in the general direction of the Asamkirche [Asam Church], a jewel of Baroque architecture on Sendlingerstrasse, passing a bookstore that featured in its window the German-born poet, novelist, painter, and much revered former Schwabing resident Hermann Hesse [1877-1962], who continues to be one of the bestselling German-speaking writers in the world.

As a schoolgirl in Germany, I had especially liked *Siddhartha* [1922] and *The Glass Bead Game* [1943], both of which deal with the theme of personal enlightenment.

Inside the bookstore, Andreas scouted for a legal thriller. I found *Siddhartha* in several translations, English among them. As I skimmed the book, I remembered teaching it in the U.S. in the 1960s. My students had identified with the generation gap issues it raises.

Around the age of twenty, Siddhartha, the protagonist, leaves his parental home to make his own way in the world. Siddhartha's father, a caring and responsible parent, is distressed that his son doesn't want to follow in his footsteps. To his credit, however, he grows to understand that ultimately Siddhartha must be allowed to choose his own path and as they part, he offers his son his blessings. Many years later, Siddhartha's own son refuses to embrace the course chosen for him by *his* father. Siddhartha had forgotten that only through disappointment, setback, and suffering had he accessed the truth for himself. Gradually he overcomes his selfish attachment to people (his son) and to things, enabling him to reach his goal: true enlightenment.

Suddenly I heard a familiar voice cry: "I found it!" Andreas flashed his legal thriller.

We then set out for the Asamkirche, as a welcome breeze began blowing and clouds massed. "We could use a spot of rain," sighed Andreas, who earlier had grumbled about Munich's notorious *Föhn,* a warm, dry, southerly wind that lasts for a full day or two. It occurs mainly in the spring, but appears at other times of the year as well.

The *Föhn* sweeps up from the Mediterranean, over the Alps and down their northern slopes. In its wake comes air so clean that some Munich residents imagine that the Alps have actually migrated to the very fringes of their city. The sky turns an azure blue, making Munich glow. Some say the *Föhn* induces migraines, others that it elevates blood pressure, still others say it makes them irritable. I can't weigh in on these symptoms, but from my time in Italy I know that the Italians have a bothersome wind, too. They call theirs the *scirocco.* It blasts hot air off the Sahara, and causes long-suffering Italians exasperation and fatigue.

At the Asamkirche, whose official name is Johann-Nepomuk-Kirche (built from 1733-46), I learned that Munich residents have long preferred that this Baroque *tour de force* be known by the names of its builders, the Asam brothers, Cosmas Damian Asam and Egid Quirin Asam.

A small Catholic church, the Asamkirche is well suited to its urban setting and is used most often for weddings. For its dimly lit nave, the Asam brothers employed all the Baroque period's flourishes to create the illusion of a transcendent world. Every surface is adorned, and on the richest, grandest theatrical scale.

During their lifetime the brothers were considered the area's most celebrated builders and decorators.

Only two other Bavarian churches have impressed me as much as the Asamkirche: the Hofkirche in Würzburg and the Wieskirche near Landsberg and Füssen, the site of Ludwig's acclaimed Neuschwanstein Castle. All three celebrate the Baroque.

Andreas numbers himself among the Bavarian Roman Catholics. He is pleased that the current pope, Benedict XVI (Joseph Alois Ratzinger), is German and was ordained in his native Bavaria on June 19, 1951.

For lunch, we had reservations at Munich's colorful Franziskaner restaurant, a ten-minute walk away. We ordered a Munich specialty: Weisswürste (white sausages) filled with veal, onion, and parsley.

Once seated in this old Munich eating establishment, we luxuriated in the Weisswürste eating ritual: The sausage casing is slit along its side, so that the meat slides out. It's then cut into bite-sized portions and eaten with sweet mustard and fresh pretzels. Andreas ordered *ein Helles* (beer) and I consumed a glass of Johannisberg Riesling.

After this interlude, we dashed to the Alte Pinakothek to view *The Four Apostles* (1526), considered by many to be Albrecht Dürer's greatest artistic achievement.

The apostles (John, Peter, Mark and Paul) appear as larger-than-life figures. Red-robed John, on the far left of the painting, exudes an air of confidence. He holds an open *New Testament* from which he reads the first verses of his famous Gospel. Slightly behind John is Peter, The Rock, to whom Jesus says, "Feed my sheep" (John: 21:17). In this rendering, Peter looks as if he has come to terms with his towering charge—to be the keeper of the key to heaven. In Mark, I saw angry eyes, but maybe they were just the impatient eyes of someone with a packed agenda. White-robed Paul, in front of Mark and to the right of the painting, seems burdened, as if tested by life. He holds a closed Gospel, an appropriate symbol for one whose writings make up a third of the *New Testament*. He leans on a sword, possibly a reference to his subsequent execution.

After our visit, Andreas went to meet his daughter and grandchildren, and I had to catch a train.

Such has been our friendship: a grand collection of brief encounters. I liked that on this occasion our time together ended in the company of Albrecht Dürer, one of Germany's most celebrated icons.

❀

Part of Munich's wonder is its proximity to the Alps—Europe's highest mountain range, though generally considered to be of "moderate" elevation. The Zugspitze, Germany's highest mountain, ascends a mere 9,700 feet, whereas Mont Blanc, the alpine chain's tallest peak, towers to an impressive 15,771 feet.

Most have heard of Garmisch-Partenkirchen and Oberammergau. They're located in what is known as the German Alps, only minutes by train or car from Munich's city center, offering a year-round recreational paradise.

I have often visited each of these high points, plus Berchtesgaden and Neuschwanstein. However, for me the alpine destination that evokes the warmest memories is Schliersee, a lake town nestled among mountain meadows and jagged limestone peaks, about an hour south of Munich. My grandparents lived there after World War II, and I spent many happy childhood vacations with them.

Now I boarded a train at Munich's Hauptbahnhof and, after experiencing much chugging and whistle-tooting, found myself transported to my childhood paradise. There my old friends Franz and Lotte Huber welcomed me as their overnight guest.

Franz and Lotte grew up in Schliersee. They were healthy, pink-cheeked teenagers when I met them in 1955, skiing in nearby Spitzingsee, a resort south of Schliersee, close to the Austrian border. Frequent gold and silver medalists, they were the envy of all who competed with them. Now they're white-haired grandparents, but their rigorous alpine life has kept them fit.

Soon after I entered college in the United States, Frank and Lotte, who were slightly older than I, fell in love and married. With training in hotel management, they eventually bought pastureland near Spitzingsee and built a lodge that to this day affords them a thriving business.

After settling into a room in their lodge, I wandered uphill a quarter-mile to their home. Two Huber dogs sounded an alarm but once they caught my scent they settled down; I had been there before.

While Lotte put the finishing touches on supper, I stretched my legs in the wildflower-filled meadow that abuts their house. Emma, a long-haired dachshund, and Rolf, a wire-haired pointer, could hardly wait to join me.

The dogs and I walked along a stream that I knew was filled with trout. We scavenged for edelweiss, gentians, anemones, and violets—typical alpine flowers—and chased butterflies. Rolf had brought his tennis ball and for several raucous minutes played fetch with me. Eventually, Emma, the all-too-serious Alpha-dog, had enough of our silliness and started to march home. Seeing this, Rolf, Emma's faithful lackey, dropped his ball and fell into line.

When we returned to the house, I saw that Lotte had prepared a generous tray of smoked and cooked meats, sausages, cheeses, and vegetables.

On two or three occasions during our supper conversation, I heard Franz and Lotte refer to "Liesi" as though they were speaking about a grandchild. When I asked about her, they recounted this:

Three years before, in the month of June, a baby deer was born in the very meadow where Emma, Rolf, and I had strolled that evening. Usually two or three comprise a deer litter, and the mother deer separates her young at birth into different parts of the meadow to hide them from foxes.

Shortly after the mother deer's delivery, the farmer who owned the meadow cut a portion of it for hay. In the process he discovered a newborn fawn, probably only three days old, totally exposed to the environment. The mother deer was nowhere in sight and nightfall was approaching. To save this little creature's life, the farmer picked it up with his hands, carried it to the nearest house—Franz and Lotte's—and asked them to take it in.

The Hubers lived in such harmony with nature that they knew that the human smell already on the fawn would cause the mother to reject it, maybe even kill it. Since they already had Emma and Rolf, they thought *what's one more?*

As soon as Lotte saw the fawn, she took it into her arms, wrapped it in a towel, prepared a warm formula from a drymilk product for dogs, and began feeding her new charge with a baby bottle, a process that continued for three months. The deer thrived and gained the name Liesi.

When Lotte and Franz retired at night, usually around 11 p.m., they took Liesi and a bottle of warm formula to bed with them. After being fed, Liesi fell into a deep sleep. But by 4 a.m., she was wide awake and wildly hungry. Then Franz would get up, heat more formula, and bring Liesi and her bottle back to bed. After her feeding, the whole family fell back to sleep until seven. "The bonding," said Franz, "was incredible."

They told me Emma and Rolf adopted her. Liesi became one of them. They protected her. "They let her sleep in their bed whenever she wanted," Lotte said.

While the young deer settled into her new foster home, her mother wandered the meadow and vicinity calling her baby—

22

for weeks. Franz and Lotte heard her sorrowful cries, but they knew she would reject Liesi if they reunited them, so they held fast to their commitment to shepherd her into maturity.

By fall, Liesi continued to live mainly indoors. The primary exception: She loved to go hunting with Franz, Emma, and Rolf.

By Christmas she was fully assimilated into family life, sitting under the Christmas tree, merrily chewing on its branches. When spring arrived, Liesi wanted to live outside. Then in late July, early August, she disappeared for two weeks. When she came back she was pregnant.

A deer's gestation lasts ten-and-a-half months. In May of the following year, Liesi delivered two fawns. She tried to bring her newborns to Franz and Lotte, but Emma, the ever-controlling dachshund, chased them off. This forced Liesi to make her life in the wild, but she made frequent, solitary visits back home to her foster family.

Two months after her fawns' birth, Liesi was shot by a hunter who then decapitated her. The Hubers' neighbor's dog, a St. Bernard with whom Liesi had played, found her head and brought it home to his master, placing it on the living room floor. The neighbor then called Franz and Lotte who collected Liesi's remains and gave her a proper burial.

"What happened to Liesi's fawns?" I asked.

"Since they had not been handled by humans, another deer adopted them," Lotte said.

When the story ended, we all sat around the dinner table in stunned silence.

To dispel the gloom, Lotte mercifully asked if anyone would like dessert, a *crostata* with goat cheese and plums she'd brought from the lodge.

"*That* you have to try," Franz insisted, "especially if it has *Schlag*" [whipping cream].

23

The dessert proved to be all that Franz had promised.

By now it was late, and Franz and the dogs accompanied me downhill to the lodge.

The next morning we fished for trout. We rode a cable car up a mountain we used to ski down together. We strolled in a nearby meadow where Emma and Rolf could accompany us. Then, late in the afternoon, Lotte and Franz took me to the train for my one-hour ride back to Munich.

While enjoying a farewell dinner with Petra and Walter in their home, I glanced across their bookshelf and saw that, as before, my sister still collects books on aphorisms. Among her authors: Erasmus of Rotterdam, Blaise Pascal—but also Benjamin Franklin and Ralph Waldo Emerson. When I asked once what fascinated her about this genre, she replied that she liked its pithy truths: "In a moment, you capture volumes." As I browsed among her collection, I opened a book of Friedrich Nietzsche's (1844-1900) sayings. I read: "*Was mich nicht umbringt, macht mich stärker*" (That which does not kill me, makes me stronger). For me, at that moment, his words encapsulated Munich's amazing spirit—to survive well over a millennium of seeking and building, only to reach the twentieth century and be confronted by such atrocities as World War I, World War II, and the 1972 Olympic massacre. But Munich endured and prevailed, becoming what some describe as the world's best city in which to live, Germany's secret capital.

24

2
Dubai

Dubayy

"Acquire knowledge. It enables its possessor to know right from wrong; it lights the way to heaven; it is our friend in the desert, our society in solitude, our companion when friendless; it guides us to happiness; it sustains us in misery; it is an ornament among friends, and an armor against enemies."
    —Inscription found on an old Arabian Peninsula door

Reflecting on his country's place in the world, Dubai's charismatic ruler, His Highness Sheikh Mohammed bin Rashid al Maktoum (1949-), told *The Wall Street Journal* (January 12, 2008) that his people have had to adapt and create anew, having been circumscribed by conflict: the Iraq-Iran war, the attack on Kuwait, and the war in Iraq. Sheikh Mohammed (who is also vice-president and prime minister of the United Arab Emirates [UAE]) is acutely aware of the need for education and entrepreneurship in a part of the world where one-and-a half-billion people live. Twenty percent of Arab youth, eighty million young people, are out of work, which His Highness views as a contributing factor in their being drawn to radicalism, often because there are no other choices.

In the early twentieth century, Dubai was little more than a forsaken fishing and pearling village. The ruling family, the

House of Maktoum, decided to boost the struggling economy by making it tax-free in order to lure entrepreneurial Iranian traders to its shores. The strategy worked, bringing not only a new vitality to this drowsy town, but also a new affluence. The 1930s saw the collapse of the much-prized pearl industry, which was, until the exportation of oil began in 1969, a crucial economic lifeline.

When regional oil exploration started in the 1950s, the emirate of Dubai had limited roads, schools, hospitals or electric lights, and hardly a building more substantial than the crumbling coral-stone-and-gypsum forts and watchtowers. But with the advent of oil revenues in the late 1960s, Dubai's then-ruler, His Highness Sheikh Rashid bin Saeed al Maktoum [1912-1990], began to fund much-needed infrastructure, thus laying the underpinnings for today's futuristic metropolis.

From the beginning Sheikh Rashid understood that Dubai's oil supply was limited and that he and his sons who would succeed him would have to build an economy that could sustain itself beyond the oil bonanza. As he famously asserted, his grandfather rode a camel, his father rode a camel, he drives a Mercedes, his son drives a Land Rover, his grandson will drive a Land Rover, but his great grandson will ride a camel.

Reverting to the past was not an option. In the desert of southern Arabia, where Sheikh Mohammed and his people were born, the past consisted of empty wastes, soul-killing heat, scorching and suffocating sand storms, and dunes the size of massifs. Hunger and thirst were steady companions as were hardship and privation. In his book, *Seven Pillars of Wisdom*, Lawrence of Arabia summed up the environment in this parched region: *[Their] ways were hard even for those brought up in them, and for strangers terrible: a death in life.*

No one who had tasted a better life wanted to return to that.

With infrastructure in place, Sheikh Rashid invested in commerce, aviation and tourism—all revenue-generating business ventures for when the oil ran out. Simultaneously, he set about developing a business-friendly environment that would attract foreign investments. Commercial agreements were largely oral, sealed with a handshake. There were no written contracts, no receipts—only one's sacred word and the threat of besmirching one's own reputation. Unfortunately, as time progressed, foreigners so often deceived Dubai's early, trusting businessmen that an unsecured commercial enterprise eventually became out of the question.

Sheikh Rashid set the stage for Dubai's electrifying rise from near-poverty to sophisticated urban giant, but the Dubai we see today is largely the creation of his third son, the previously mentioned British-educated Sheikh Mohammed.

As I write, Dubai's freewheeling capitalist ways have been chastened by the 2008-2009 global financial crisis. Some describe this downturn as nothing more than a "cold snap" for the emirate's otherwise robust economy; others say it is far more serious. Be that as it may, these reflections highlight what I found wondrous—even heroic—about Dubai and the UAE in general: the land's stunning ascent from parched, quasi-medieval hinterland to economic powerhouse with one of the highest standards of living in the world. In just a few decades the home-grown people of Dubai and environs, commonly called the Emiratis, "the nationals" or simply "the locals," joined the ranks of the richest and best-educated people in the world, with a life expectancy better than our own—all thanks to oil.

In the mid-1970s, my then-husband served as an economic advisor to the ruler of a neighboring emirate. From 1976 to 1978, I spent the better part of each year in and around Dubai proper, which was an easy fifteen-minute drive from our home. Since then I have revisited Dubai, marveling at the changes that have transpired in a single generation.

On my first visit, the bleached yellow land looked as if solar rays had penetrated the earth itself. And they had, cutting deep cracks in the terrain. The immense sky, usually stark blue and cloudless, changed color only at dawn and sunset.

In those days Dubai consisted mainly of one and two-story structures. Occasionally, newly built mosques punctuated the landscape, as did wide boulevards, roundabouts, and modern lighting. But apart from these early signs of new wealth, remnants of another age—makeshift shantytowns, mud-brick huts, and shacks made from palm fronds—were tucked along the side roads.

It was as common to encounter goats, sheep, and camels on the roads as cars, and all too easy to find oneself about to crash into animals. Camels were particularly lethal. Many a driver was killed instantly colliding with an ambling "ship of the desert." Clearly, Dubai was a land in radical transition.

In January 1976, when I landed at the Dubai International Airport for the first of several lengthy stays, I arrived with Champ, our much loved ninety-pound, long-haired, honey-colored collie. (My husband David was already there.) During the unloading procedure, Champ's kennel fell the equivalent of two stories from the belly of our 747 onto the tarmac. The kennel literally exploded. Miraculously, Champ was not hurt but, terror-struck, he fled for his life. No one had a chance to stop him. He was bent on getting as far away as possible from the nightmare of airport sounds and sights.

Instead of seeking people or someplace with water and food, he struck out into the open desert that abuts the *Rub'al Khali*, the so-called Empty Quarter of the Arabian Peninsula. This is the largest continuous body of sand in the world, a belt

28

of salt flats and shifting dunes the size of Texas, which even the Bedouins, the traditional desert dwellers, find daunting. Daytime summer temperatures easily reach 130° F, and in winter, the night temperature drops well below freezing. With good reason, Lawrence of Arabia called this inhospitable terrain "a death in life." And that's where Champ reportedly was headed.

Initially, David and I searched for Champ on our own, but after a full day without success we reported the airport accident to the Dubai police. They agreed to distribute fliers to their police force describing Champ and advertising our reward. We also contacted the Dubai media—all were willing to help.

Meanwhile, on the fifth day of our loss, Sheikh Mohammed, who was known throughout the Gulf as a sportsman, was in the desert flying his falcons. Falconry was a particular passion of his, one he often practiced near an oasis called Al-Aweer, about thirty-five kilometers from Dubai's center. As he marched along, he suddenly noticed fresh animal tracks in the sand. Though he is Western-educated, his traditions are distinctly Bedouin. Historically, Bedouins have been known as superb trackers with an uncanny ability to follow trails over miles of harsh terrain.

Sheikh Mohammed later told us that he knew the tracks were only about a half-hour old and not those of a native animal. Curious, he decided to follow them. Within half an hour he found Champ, who was by then ragged, thin, exhausted, near death.

The Qur'an teaches that man has a duty to animals. In Jasser's translation, it says, "All the animals that roam the earth and all the birds that fly in the sky are formed in communities like your own. We have left nothing out from the Book, and they shall all be assembled to God" [6:38].* Hospitality, particularly in the desert, is a stringent duty. Champ was a wanderer lost,

---

*Mohamed K. Jasser, *The Holy Qur'an: An Interpretive Translation from Classical Arabic into Contemporary English* [Arizona: Arcadia Publishing, Inc. 2008], 84.

a stranger, to whom refusing hospitality would have been an affront to God.

"This must be the dog that was lost at the Dubai Airport last week," one of the Sheikh's aides said.

Sheikh Mohammed took Champ to the oasis for food and water. He gave him shelter, a shiny new collar, comfort and hope. And a day or two later, in a beautiful ceremony, he returned Champ to us. At the close of the formal proceeding, I shook the Sheikh's hand. "How can I ever thank you?"

"*Maalaysh*," [It was nothing], he said, with the smile of a man long-practiced in the art of kindness.

The Sheikh was then the minister of defense, a position he assumed in 1971, just after the founding of the United Arab Emirates [UAE]. After he returned Champ to us, I made it a point to find out more about him. From all sides I heard only praise. Only twenty-two years old, the youngest minister of defense in the world, he was described as a humanitarian, a hero to children, an animal-lover, a pilot, a prince.

Today he rules a nation and is lauded as a key architect of Dubai's transformation from a sleepy desert enclave with a few hundred thousand inhabitants to a micro-kingdom that bristles with initiative.

Among Sheikh Mohammed's many initiatives was his ten billion-dollar gift, in 2007, to establish the Sheikh Mohammed bin Rashid al-Maktoum Foundation. With this endowment, he hoped to enhance his region's standard of education and research to spark job creation in the Middle East. He told BBC News that he desired to create a knowledge-based society. This reflected his understanding that there is a huge knowledge divide between his part of the world and the developed West and Asia. In some parts of the Middle East, more than forty percent of Arab women still cannot read or write, and the whole of the Arab world publishes fewer books than does Turkey. His region needed fifteen million jobs, he said, anticipating that in twenty years as many as eighty-five million jobs would be required.

From my time among the Emiratis, I learned that devout Muslims believe God is the source of all things and that understanding creation helps them to understand Him better. A true believer sees books and knowledge as spiritual nourishment, and by learning, he or she is seeking God. So it makes sense from all perspectives that education has been a priority since the founding of the United Arab Emirates in 1971.

Often called a blend of Singapore and Las Vegas, Dubai is a tiny sovereign state of just 1,588.4 square miles (about the size of Rhode Island). It has a population of about one-and-a-half million of whom only about fifteen percent are indigenous.

Since 1971, Dubai (the emirate of Dubai and its main city carry the same name) has been the second largest of the seven loosely federated states (Abu Dhabi, Dubai, Sharjah, Ras al-Khaimah, Fujairah, Umm al-Qaiwain, and Ajman) that comprise the United Arab Emirates. The UAE borders the Gulf of Oman and the Persian Gulf (known to Arabs as the Arabian Gulf), lying just east of Saudi Arabia and west of Oman. Bahrain and Qatar, though invited to join the union, chose to remain outside. While each state maintains a large amount of independence, a Supreme Council of Rulers, made up of seven emirs who appoint the prime minister and cabinet, governs the UAE in such matters as foreign affairs, defense, social services, and immigration.

A bastion of stability in the often strife-ridden Middle East, the UAE is also a staunch ally of the U.S., supporting both Gulf wars and the so-called war on terror.

Dubai has traditionally shown itself able to make the most of its environment. Since earliest recorded times, this Middle Eastern settlement was a hub for eastern and western Silk Road traders. As early as A.D. 800, Gulf merchants were trading with India, Ceylon, the East Indies and China in such prized goods as spices, silks, ivory, aromatics, wood, paper, and saddlery.

Dubai attributes its initial fortunes to the "Creek," an 8.7-mile inlet from the Arabian Gulf that allowed this seemingly forsaken community to become a strategic and profitable port of call. While sandbars tended to form around the entrance of the Creek, obstructing the passage of large oceangoing vessels, they also pacified the tides, creating quiet oyster beds that proved ideal habitats for pearling—the economic lifeline I mentioned earlier.

In the sixteenth century, Dubai gained international acclaim by exporting locally harvested pearls to India and Europe. The Venetian jeweler Gasparo Balbi is believed to have been the first to make written reference to "Dibei" in describing his 1580 expedition to uncover new sources of precious gems.

It was also around this time that European powers such as Portugal, Holland, and eventually Britain tried to dominate the profitable trade routes, which sprang from this region. For a time they succeeded in taxing the Gulf's trade with India and the Far East.

As these foreign influences waned, the Qawasim, a federation of Arab tribes governed by the Qasimi family, grew in prominence by imposing tolls on foreign vessels passing through the Straits of Hormuz, that twenty-nine-mile-wide choke point of the Gulf through which about sixteen to seventeen million barrels of oil now pass each day.

The British East India Company came into conflict with the Qawasim over these tolls, and from 1805-1811, the British government defeated the tribes in a series of raids. In due course, the British and nine regional sheikhdoms signed a number of treaties, intended to preserve a maritime truce, after which the region came to be called The Trucial States.

That the British chose to "protect" rather than colonize the emirates enabled them to retain internal sovereignty, thus preserving their old ways. The British controlled only the Trucial States' foreign affairs and defense. As a consequence, social development (health, education, labor, etc.) languished until the discovery of oil. But once awash in oil, the rulers pursued social development with a vengeance.

While living in the UAE, I studied Arabic with Abdulla, a language teacher, who like many Dubaians had an easy manner and smiled readily. I couldn't guess his age, but surmised that he was younger than he looked. The sun had dug deep trenches in his dark-complexioned face. He spoke distinctly British English, a legacy, I suspected, from the protectorship years that ended in 1971.

He taught me that Arabic stems from a Semitic tradition and is spoken by more than two hundred million people in more than twenty countries, and is read from right to left.

I learned that people who call themselves Arabs are generally linked by language, but there are countless dialects and some are not understood from one Arab land to another. While most of our one-hour tutorials focused on grammar, midway through our lessons a server brought us coffee (*qahwah*). Always Abdulla would interrupt his instruction to take a sip, relishing the last of the cardamom seeds at the bottom of the cup. After his caffeine rush, he became animated and his nimble mind jumped onto a track that we both enjoyed more than our usual drill.

During breaks I enjoyed gazing around his office, with its piles of books, stacks of papers, a rickety typewriter, and a diverse array of tribal artifacts: camel saddle, loom, Bedouin fiddle, and brass coffeepots in varying sizes. On the walls and floor lay masses of plaited rugs in brown and white bands with accents of red, orange, and light blue. These objects almost always prompted us to talk about the Bedouins, of whom Abdulla was a proud descendent.

"Some Arabs believe that the Bedouins are the only truly moral people remaining among us," Abdulla said one day, adding that the concept of personal honor or "face" had long been considered a key virtue to which desert dwellers aspired. It is attained by being brave, generous, virile (producing many sons), and by possessing pure bloodlines. Abdulla said that even today many settled Arabs throughout the Middle East see the Bedouin way of life as ideal, and many profess Bedouin blood, even though in the 1970s technically only about ten percent were bona fide Bedouins.

Today in the UAE about one hundred eighty thousand are said to be Bedouins and they are generally divided into two classes: the true Bedouin, the nomadic shepherds, who are committed to the wanderer's life and instinctively resist anything imposed by outside authorities, and the *fellahin* who have long lived on the periphery of the desert, straddling both worlds. Already in the 1970s, young Bedouin men took jobs in towns, often in the oil industry, but went home to their Bedouin camps on weekends. Abdulla sometimes mused about their patriarchal culture: "What's funny is that these days women often earn more money than men by selling their crafts in town." He said that some Bedouins who didn't want to be a part of settled communities earned respectable livelihoods by breeding camels for racing, sometimes tending their herds with the latest-model pickup trucks. Fast forwarding to the twenty-first century, most Bedouins in the UAE have become urbanized Arabs; by law their children are required to attend school until the age of sixteen.

The Bedouins' desert existence could not have happened without the domestication of the camel some three thousand years ago. Its padded feet act almost like snowshoes in the shifting sand. More critically, the camel has the capacity to go for long stretches without water. On cooler days it can survive for about twenty-five days without a drink; in hot weather, about five days. Old-timers say that in dire circumstances they sometimes jammed a stick down a camel's throat to make it regurgitate. If the camel had drunk water within the last two days, the regurgitated liquid would be tolerably drinkable. To illustrate the camel's importance to desert life, Abdulla said that the Arabic language contains about a thousand words depicting the camel in its various states of being. This number is trumped only by variations of the word "sword."

The Bedouins passed on to their descendents many legacies, among them the aforementioned sense of hospitality, which was the paramount law of the desert. Without it, people traveling in the wilderness away from their own communities would die. Over time it became customary to extend hospitality even to strangers for an obligatory three days. During this time a visitor would not be required to state his name or business; he was simply received. The poorest of hosts would then offer his last bit of food to his guest.

The traditional attitude toward hospitality in the desert is best conveyed by this proverb:

O guest of ours though you have come, though you have visited us, though you have honored our dwelling, we verily are the real guests and you are lord of this house.

Once during our coffee break, Addulla introduced me to Salman, a colleague and refugee from Lebanon's then-raging civil war. Salman mentioned that he missed his native village in the hills above Beirut where his aging mother lived. I asked why he didn't go back to visit her.

"Because I'd get shot," Salman answered unhesitatingly.

I must have looked astonished, because he explained immediately that he had been the principal of a school there and in that role, he had had to fire a few people. If he were to go back now, some mysterious, untraceable, sniper bullet would in all probability find him. It would come from the son, brother, or maybe even a nephew of one of the people he had fired. "You've heard of an eye for an eye and a tooth for a tooth—the law of retaliation or revenge killing?" he asked.

I nodded.

While the desert offered the Bedouin freedom, in its harsh environment only the rugged survived. Without a central government, the Bedouins had no choice but to depend first on family and then on tribal cohesion for self-protection. Abdulla shared with me an esteemed Bedouin saying: *I and my brothers against my cousins; I and my cousins against the stranger.* In this culture the group matters more than the individual.

The family unit was held responsible for the actions of any one of its members. Crime was deterred by the fear of lasting retribution. Those who brought harm to another could expect to be harmed.

One of Abdulla's most memorable gifts to me was introducing me to Melek, who, along with her husband, was also a refugee from Beirut's civil war, in which their young son died amid the factional fighting. In both Beirut and Dubai, they were teachers.

Melek had been educated at the American University of Beirut, founded by American missionaries in 1866 as the Syrian Protestant College. Now in Dubai she tutored me in the Middle East's literary tradition, especially the prose.

While scholarship had long prospered in Mesopotamia

and later in Islamic Spain (see the chapter entitled "Andalusia"), little had filtered down to the tribes of the Arabian Peninsula, whose members included the inhabitants of what is now the UAE. Geographical isolation clearly was a factor. Except for the privileged, who could travel abroad to study, inhabitants of the Arabian Peninsula had to wait until the discovery of oil and the formation of their own self-sustaining union to obtain universal education. Until then, their lives revolved around food, shelter and family. Most knew little beyond their ancient customs, beliefs (often consisting of *hadiths*, the teachings and actions traced back to Prophet Mohammed as recorded by his close associates) and injunctions learned from the Qur'an. They were not planners and recorders. Still close to their nomadic past, they had the habits of desert tribesmen who needed no ledgers. Of necessity their values centered on intangibles, on ideas stored in men's memories.

Emiratis have long commemorated significant occasions with language—especially poetry.

As Islam expanded across the Middle East and non-Arabs embraced it as a religion, these non-Arabs began to speak some Arabic, a version different from Classical Arabic (the language in which the Qur'an is written, considered by many to be a sacred or divine language). Their Arabic became known as *Nabati,* sometimes called *Bint al rimal* (daughter of the sands). Melek was a student of this type of poetry and delighted in telling me about it.

Derived from Classical Arabic, Nabati poetry depicts in colloquial or vernacular speech, the realities of everyday life, primarily on the Arabian Peninsula. Nabati dates back to the sixteenth century and is now seen as an important resource for historians as they study the Arabian Peninsula.

Sheikh Mohammed is also a serious student of Nabati poetry. Initially, he published his writings under pseudonyms

37

for fear that the media would print his verses only because he was a member of the ruling family. But critics recognized his talent—and today he's broadly acknowledged as one of the world's finest Nabati poets. He now publishes under his own name. His favorite theme deals with wisdom.

Melek rarely alluded to herself. Her focus was outward: "How are you today?" and "What do you think?" among her favorite expressions. I liked her eyes—shining but sad—eyes that knew a lot but kept a lot inside. As I watched her, I sometimes wished that she could bring herself to cry. But that was not her way, not the desert way, where courage and stoicism were hallowed virtues. Nevertheless, one day the floodgates opened.

She spoke of her grief at losing her son, Karam, during Beirut's civil war, and her regret at having been so caught up in her work when he was young that she spent too little time nuturing him. He had seemed self-sufficient, but he wasn't; he was only a child. In 1975 he was killed after school by a stray bullet while she was at work. Melek's mother, who was caring for him, had given him permission to ride his bike. Forever, Melek berated herself for not being home.

Maybe then, she thought, the bullet would not have found him. If there is a silver lining in losing a child ("And that," she said, "is a big if") perhaps it is that the experience has brought her a deeper appreciation of life itself: its wonder and beauty and joy and the blessing of having had Karam even for just a few years. She said losing him reminded her how fragile our lives are.

As Melek and I parted that day, an Arab proverb I had just come across seemed apt:

Who is your favorite child? The youngest one, until he is grown up; the absent one, until he comes back; the sick one, until he recovers.

After an absence of twenty-five years, my port of entry was again Dubai International Airport. It had mushroomed from serving about nine airlines with twenty destinations in the 1970s to one that accommodated nearly a hundred airlines with more than two hundred destinations.

As I took my first steps on the airport carpet patterned after wind-blown desert sands, I found myself engulfed in a forest of indoor palm trees interspersed with lavish duty-free shops full of gold jewelry, DVD players, and designer brands; I even glimpsed a Starbucks. Strolling beside me were throngs of humanity—Arabs, Indians, Asians, Africans, and Europeans, a universe in microcosm. *If only we were all so well-behaved and peaceable in our respective corners,* I thought to myself.

I remembered reading that this facility was built in 1998 for $540 million and allowed visitors to proceed from plane to street in a mere twelve minutes. The airport's efficiency proved to be just as advertised.

Outdoors I was struck all over again by the brilliant Gulf light—and the heat. I'd forgotten how early in the day—it was only about eight in the morning—one can feel as if one were in a sauna.

As my taxi headed toward the city center, I saw through the morning haze a spectacular skyline of towering steel and blue glass structures. I felt completely disoriented. In the 1970s I knew every nook and cranny of Dubai—it was just a small town. Now I saw stately edifices of sand-colored stone, which I would later come to know as government buildings and museums. I saw a virtual forest of construction cranes, which some like to joke should be Dubai's national bird. Today Dubai's skyline includes the imposing Burj Khalifa, a solitary, slender needle reaching 2,717 feet into the sky—currently the world's tallest man-made structure.

When I first returned, I was immediately struck by the landscaping—acres of lawns, flower beds and well-tended palm trees, all irrigated by Gulf water run through desalination plants. I was reminded once again how far these people had come from the grave world of dunes and sandbars I'd known only a few decades earlier. At the same time, I was impressed with how fastidiously they cared for their environment, now that they had the resources. As of 2008, Sheikh Mohammed has decreed that all new buildings must be constructed according to the highest international environment-friendly standards. Dubai has thus become the first city in the Middle East and one of the first in the world to turn green.

Dubai's inhabitants, like most UAE citizens, appear content with their lives in this benign autocracy that assures them free education, health care, and study-abroad opportunities. No cry for western-style democracy here! These people enjoy their own form of democracy: the *majlis* (an Arabic term that means "place of sitting" or assembly; we might call it a town hall-type of gathering) which ties in well with the quranic principles of consultation and consensus. When citizens have a complaint, they attend a *majlis* conducted by a senior royal, where, regardless of their station in life, they are free to express their concerns. To avert any hint of unrest, the ruling family responds quickly to whatever issue a citizen might bring up. (The *majlis* concept, common to all the federated emirates, proves feasible because of the small native-born population; only Emiratis are eligible to participate.)

After settling into my hotel, I called Yasmin and Aziz, my Dubai friends from the 1970s with whom I'd remained in touch all these years. They were out but I was assured they would be back soon.

When I heard the word "soon," I recalled my early struggles with the Arab concept of time: External forces, definitely not man, control time. For those who are devout Muslims, this does not suggest that God pre-ordains all things, but a prudent believer operates under the assumption that God might have already initiated a series of circumstances that affect future time. It would, therefore, be presumptuous for man to take the initiative in organizing time. He can *attempt* to organize it, with the understanding that at any moment something unforeseen could intervene.

Since I was too excited to sleep, I decided to taxi to the famed Burj Al Arab Hotel, the Tower of the Arabs. Its sail, I was told, made of double-skinned, Teflon-coated fiberglass, was intended to remind us of the region's seafaring tradition, especially its dhow trading vessels. In *City of Gold,* however, Jim Krane suggests a grander objective: It was to be "the most significant Arab monument since the Alhambra." Built in the fourteenth century for the last Muslim Emirs in Spain, the Moorish palaces of the Alhambra are a magnificent testament to Islamic architecture and a major tourist attraction.

Metal detectors with security agents, who profiled guests and visitors, greeted me at the hotel entrance. "Why all this?" I asked. "To provide security for the delegates of an international conference in session here," I was told.

Once in the lobby, I felt steeped in opulence, as if Beverly Hills' Rodeo Drive and the Bellagio in Las Vegas had collided. Art galleries display modern and traditional art. Shop windows display miniature palm trees and camels made of gold. I saw jewels that any crowned head of Europe would covet.

The lavish jewels and art objects are not on sale for foreign visitors exclusively; behind the veil many Arab women dress in high style, and Arab homes are often museums of priceless art. None of this is prohibited by the Qur'an. Only to flaunt that which is beautiful is problematic, because doing so could create envy—in the eyes of many *a sickness of soul and heart,* as Melek said. She shared a traditional Islamic saying: "Beware of envy because indeed envy destroys good deeds in the same manner as fire destroys wood."

After strolling through the lobby, past waterfall cascades and aquariums so big that staff have to wear scuba gear to clean them, I took another taxi, this time to the Gold Souq. En route I saw exotic birds, likely finding temporary refuge on the Dubai Creek Golf Course or in the Khor Dubai Wildlife Sanctuary. Indeed, the Arabian Gulf is the migratory crossroads for billions of birds as they migrate from Central Asia through Arabia to winter in Africa.

When I first lived in and around Dubai, I couldn't imagine becoming enamored with my new physical environment. It seemed too alien, too barren. But on walks along the beach with Champ, I grew to like standing at the water's edge, feeling the sand between my toes and listening to the rollers come pounding in. Seashells—the spiny murek, augur shells, scallops and cockles—were the first of the Gulf's natural wonders to preoccupy me. And Champ frolicked with gulls and terns as they scavenged for food on the beach or plunged like kamikazes into the Gulf for fish. Briefly he imagined he could outrun them, but their speed and dexterity outmaneuvered him every time. It thrilled me to think that the small birds that sometimes rested in our shrubbery might have traveled all the way from Siberia.

I liked knowing that just beyond the water's edge sea-creatures such as green turtles, dugongs, and dolphins made their home. I grew to rejoice in the dolphin's sociability, its tendency to cling to its mother for years, to hunt for food in packs, its fondness for human contact. I delighted in the dolphins' leaps of joy, their smiling faces.

When my taxi driver dropped me in the Souq, I explored

the maze of four hundred storefronts, dripping with gold necklaces, watches, earrings, brooches, and rings. My goal was to find a pair of eighteen-carat gold earrings. When I located exactly what I wanted, I bargained and settled on a price. After the merchant had swiped my credit card, he asked me what I do. "I'm an author," I said. "I plan to write about Dubai—I'm here to do research."

"If I had known you were an author," he smiled and said, "I would have given you a better price. I want you to write well of our people."

"Could we renegotiate the sale?" I proposed in fun.

"No, madam, the charge has gone through."

Actually, I was satisfied with the bargain I had made.

Former President Bill Clinton, a favorite guest speaker in Dubai, was there during the first of my return visits. A local newspaper reported his saying: "The UAE is a model for a genuine Arab, Islamic nation that houses all cultures and nationalities." It was on this occasion that he announced his foundation's sponsorship of scholarships for young Americans to study at the American University of Dubai to learn about the culture of the region. He sees Dubai as an ideal partner for bridging the gap of cultural understanding between America and the Arab world.

As I strolled through the Gold Souq labyrinth, my long Seattle-London-Dubai flight began to catch up with me. I was fading. I realized, though, that my twenty-five hours of travel was but a pittance compared to the twenty-one days an average steamship passage took from New York to the eastern shores of the Mediterranean in the 1830s, when Americans first became serious explorers of the Middle East. My fatigue seemed a small price to pay to experience the charge I felt in returning to a place I had known in its infancy and could now experience in its prime.

When I reached my hotel room to take a nap, I found a

message from Yasmin.

Yasmin is Lebanese-born, a trained historian specializing in Phoenician studies, who in the 1970s married Aziz, a native Dubaian who made his living in the oil industry. When I first met them, they had a toddler of two. Now they have three adult sons, all Cambridge educated, one with a postgraduate degree from Harvard.

Because my time in Dubai was relatively short, we decided to meet that evening for dinner at Le Royal Meridien on Al Sufouh Road.

After a separation of too many years, it was wonderful to sit face-to-face with my friends of long ago: Yasmin, petite and trim, still had her high-cheekboned Nefertiti-look, framed by rich brown hair. Like me, she now needed glasses to read the dinner menu. And Aziz, with his olive-toned skin and probing eyes, now had a head of hair as white as snow.

I still detected a powerful chemistry between the two, the fortuitous consequence of a marriage arranged by their respective parents in the mid-1970s. Aziz gave Yasmin his full attention when she spoke. He attributes their children's academic success to her careful supervision of their homework.

Although Aziz has done well in the oil industry, the centerpiece of their life together seemed to rest with their children. Our dinner conversation focused initially on their hilarious memories of Badr as a baby, who was once inadvertently locked in his room by his babysitter, along with the keys.

As the evening progressed, I asked Yasmin why the women of Dubai (and the UAE in general) seek education so zealously (more women than men here pursue higher education and they get better grades!). She said that compensates for the years they lived without the rewards that come from *ilm* (knowledge). Princess Haya, Sheikh Mohammed's wife, for example, graduated with a B.A. Honours degree in Politics, Philosophy, and Economics from the University of Oxford.

Aziz added that most children and their parents are now computer literate and have computers in their homes. "It's the grandparents who haven't caught up," he said. He reminded me that in the 1970s, the illiteracy rate in the UAE was above seventy percent; today it's less than seven percent. Ninety-nine percent of the UAE's girls attend school. Adult education classes are flourishing, rapidly bringing computer and literacy skills even to the older generations.

Today's challenge is to find jobs for all these educated women. Most UAE women work in government, in the health and education sectors. Forty-seven percent of government employees are women. The year 2004 marked an important milestone: California-educated, Her Excellency Sheikha [Princess] Lubna al-Qasimi became the first woman to be appointed to a UAE cabinet position. As I write, she is the Minister of Foreign Trade, and three other women hold cabinet posts.

To the women of the UAE, Sheikha Lubna symbolizes what is possible. After earning a Bachelor's Degree in Computer Science from California State University [Chico] in 1981, Sheikha Lubna returned to the UAE to work as a computer programmer, eventually automating the operations of the entire federal government and becoming the highly successful managing director of a major electronics firm. Her stature is such that *Forbes Magazine* named her one of the "100 Most Powerful Women in the World." In 2005 she was even nominated for a Nobel Peace Prize. Along with fulfilling her official duties, she lectures throughout the world on economic, gender, and equality issues. She hopes for the day "when gender or nationality doesn't matter—the first step toward truly achieving peace."

Finding husbands for UAE women has also become a

growing concern. To the dismay of parents, many UAE men choose not to marry women who are better educated than they. They often take foreign wives instead. Contributing to this trend of marrying "out" is the high dowry that fathers demand for their daughters—sometimes approaching one hundred thousand dollars or more. This was an issue during the 1970s when I lived there, and still is. The bride-price is often unaffordable, thus driving potential husbands to seek wives in Lebanon, Egypt, or Pakistan, where many fathers accept smaller settlements.

What is the fate of women who don't marry in a culture that enshrines marriage as their ultimate fulfillment? In extended families, single women historically became revered aunties, companions, or household helpers. Some women compromise, believing the old adage, "It's better to have a husband of wood than remain an old maid." And some become second wives, or co-wives, although now polygamy is rare. But today many single women with advanced education become self-supporting career women. Even they, however, stay close to their family's circle. Given the apparent emancipation of Dubai's women, I was surprised that they still covered themselves in *hijab.** In the 1970s I'd felt this practice might soon fade; people of the Gulf seemed eager to embrace the West then. Now, as if to defy the West, nearly every indigenous woman wears the black *abaya* [cloak] with *shayla* [head covering].

According to Yasmin, "It means nationalism." For some, the *hijab* symbolizes religious and cultural pride. Later another acquaintance explained, "It's a salute to tradition. Why should we do what the West wants us to do?" She went on to say that social pressure—from families or employers who see it as

---

*Head covering worn by Muslim women. Literally, the word means to cover or veil.

46

socially and professionally expedient—also contributes to the continued practice. "For some, *hijab* implies a sisterhood," she said. "It's about membership in an exclusive club, a network that helps you get things done. In the end it also casts a safety net over a woman. No man would dare bother a female in *hijab*."

When our conversation touched on the West's misconception of the Arab people, Aziz said, "I blame our society for its ignorance. When we go outside, we don't present ourselves."

Even though my visit occurred well after September 11, 2001, Aziz seemed to need to refer to that dreadful day by expressing his regret, assuring me that such aggression is anathema to Islam's most sacred teachings. "No matter how angry someone might be toward U.S. foreign policy," he said, "violence should never be an option." Both he and Yasmin sat silently for a moment. Then Yasmin added reflectively, "Do the actions of a few ever really define the mind of the whole?"

While today Dubai spins heads with its architectural feats—buildings of record-setting heights and new standards of luxury and entertainment—I learned from my hosts that in the 1990s a movement got underway to preserve, restore, and honor traditional Dubai. Some opposed the grandiose, brazen and modern buildings. Yasmin laughed, saying "*Vanity Fair* summed up the madness by referring to Dubai's skyline as one 'on crack.'"

New construction began to reflect an "Arabian-chic." Surviving neighborhoods are restored so that visitors can explore traditional local architecture, artifacts, and home life as they were 150 years ago, just as Americans can visit Colonial Williamsburg in Virginia. Both Yasmin and Aziz are purist in things architectural; they say that these days if you want to see authentic examples of traditional Gulf architecture, you have to travel to Oman.

47

Aziz's take on Dubai's stunning evolution is that while he's all for progress, he, along with most Dubaians, struggle with the city's nightmarish traffic. "But, as usual, Sheikh Mohammed, our great problem solver, has a solution. He's building Dubai Metro, a driverless, fully automated system of transportation, running underground in the city center and elsewhere on double-tracked elevated viaducts."

Aziz mentioned complaints by non-unionized South Asian construction workers about bad working conditions and low pay. Yet even in this arena, Dubai's ruling family has stepped in to enforce the country's labor laws more stringently and to institute reforms. Both Aziz and Yasmin spoke about Dubai's effort to balance traditional Islamic values with modernity. "Some conservative Muslims complain about Dubai's liberal ways, such as the use of alcohol in certain settings," Aziz said, "but these same individuals know that oil and gas are running out and that tourism is an essential new source of revenue. To keep millions of visitors coming, the ruling family has simply decided to offer certain amenities in addition to sunshine. Traditional Dubaians go along, although, in many cases, reluctantly."

As for progress as a center for learning and the arts, there are the Harvard affiliated Dubai School of Government, Michigan State's presence, and the Paris' Sorbonne in the neighboring emirate of Abu Dhabi. Aziz brought to mind Sheikh Mohammed's ten-billion-dollar gift to improve the Emirate's quality of education and research. "Generally, though, we're still a work in progress," he said. "It takes years to self-actualize. We've only been digging our way out of the sand since 1971." He urged me to keep coming back. "Check on our progress!" Yasmin nodded, adding that locally it's commonly bandied about that Sheikh Mohammed aspires to make Dubai the world's new Córdoba, which, in tenth century Muslim Spain was the world's greatest center of learning and tolerance. "Those are lofty ambitions, but why not aim high? I think shooting for the moon is in Sheikh Mohammed's DNA."

❀

In spite of Yasmin's reservations, she joined me early the next morning in a walk through one of Dubai's heritage areas—Bastakiya, restored and pedestrianized to showcase traditional local architecture. There I learned that over a hundred years ago, this neighborhood was the home of the Iranian traders I mentioned early in this chapter. Their abodes were made of coral and crowned with wind towers that served as natural air-conditioners, a concept they carried with them from Iran.

Today Bastakiya's wind towers are ornamental, but in the past these roofed structures had vents on all four sides that captured wind from whichever direction it blew. The tower's interior was partitioned to let cool air flow in and warm air flow out.

"If it was 105° F outside," Yasmin said, "wind towers could easily create a climate of 50° F inside." She added that ecologists are now studying this ancient cooling system, aiming for buildings with low energy demands.

In Bastakiya, we also visited the Dubai Museum, located in the Al Fahidi Fort, the town's oldest building, built in 1787. This complex of coral-and-shell rubble, once a sea defense against bellicose neighboring tribes, a seat of government, a ruler's residence, a store for ammunition, and a jail, opened as a museum in 1971 to highlight Dubai's traditional life.

We lingered longest in the part devoted to musical instruments, with a display of drums, flutes, lyres, and goatskin bagpipes used for festive occasions, a few of which I had experienced in the 1970s.

The bagpipe, my favorite local instrument, consists of tanned goatskin onto which three pipes have been installed—one to bring air into the goatskin, another to provide a continuous low tone (some say monotonous), and the third to sing the melody. The performance of makeshift instruments by musicians in flowing white *dishdashas* (robes) makes for a colorful spectacle.

After our Bastakiya visit, Yasmin invited me for lunch at her home, which was being built when I lived in the UAE.

A traditional Islamic house addresses interior spaces more readily than exterior ones. Typically, Islamic facades and doorways reveal little of what lies within. Architects describe this as "hidden architecture": Only when one enters the house is its architectural design apparent.

Yasmin's home was a flat-roofed, two-story brick house tucked behind windowless walls high enough to ensure that nothing behind them could be seen from the street. This penchant for domestic privacy springs from the seclusion and segregation of women prescribed in the Qur'an.

An electronic device opened a gate into the interior courtyard, paved in tiles and richly planted with vines and shrubbery. A fountain gushed at its center. After stepping out of her car, Yasmin said, "We call this courtyard our home's heart and lungs. It offers light, fresh air, a place for children to play and for us to be with family and friends." I noticed that all the rooms of the house opened into the central courtyard.

In the Qur'an, paradise is portrayed as a shaded and enclosed garden where water flows and ablutions before prayer are believed to purify the supplicant. In ancient times the well of Zamzam near the Ka'ba in Mecca is said to have miraculously provided surging water at the feet of Ishmael, the first son of Abraham, when his mother, Hagar, sought this life-giving element.

In Yasmin's living room, I saw books and handsome metalwork—an elegant ewer inlaid with silver arabesque, pottery with abstract designs in cobalt blue, canisters of enameled glass, and an array of oriental carpets. Yasmin pointed to a picture of

Cairo's Al-Azhar University, founded in the tenth century and still the world's most famous Islamic university, specializing in philosophy and theology. She showed me a book about the Persian Islamic scholar Ibn Sina (980-1037), known in the West as Avicenna, who wrote about medicine and philosophy, often building on the works of the ancients Greeks. I saw a replica of an astrolabe, an instrument that measures the stars' angle above the horizon, allowing the user to calculate latitude—a tool useful for worshipers who face Mecca during prayer.

Our luncheon table was framed on two sides by well-furnished bookshelves. Prasad, from India, a long-time family employee, brought us *samakah harrah* (baked fish with walnut and pomegranate stuffing) and *tabbouleh* (crushed wheat, tomato, mint and parsley salad). We talked about Yasmin's sons and her family in Lebanon. But she also asked about the United States. She and Aziz had often traveled to England, occasionally to New York and Boston while visiting their son at Harvard. When it was time for dessert, Prasad presented us with *farareer* (baked "bird's nest" pastry), embellished with nuts and syrup.

I liked the graciousness of Yasmin's life, in which she made time to invest in friendship, to share her culture with a foreigner, and to keep at bay the isolation that so often infests the West. And I liked how Dubai has begun to share its good fortune: As noted earlier, Sheikh Mohammed also spoke of embarking on a different kind of war, one that would help alleviate poverty, promote education, and foster economic development—all catalysts for self-esteem.

As our luncheon drew to a close, Yasmin presented me with the gift of a book titled *Phoenix Rising: The United Arab Emirates—Past, Present and Future* by Werner Forman.

According to Yasmin, archaeologists suggest that the idea of the phoenix may have come from a large heron that lived on the Arabian Gulf some five thousand years ago. Apparently, early traders observed the heron's brilliant scarlet and gold plumage, maybe even heard its melodic cry, and then returned to their homes, fueling the lore about its majesty.

Yasmin went on to say that the phoenix was thought to be a mythological bird, one that never dies, flying far ahead of the flock, scanning the horizon, gathering intelligence.

Only one phoenix existed at a time, with a lifespan ranging from five hundred to twelve thousand years. When the bird felt death approaching, it would build a pyre of aromatic branches and spices, perhaps cinnamon and myrrh, set it afire, and then allow itself to be consumed by the flames. After three days a new phoenix would arise from the ashes.

"The legend might have had something to do with the ancient world's longing for immortality," Yasmin said. Then the early Christians interpreted the phoenix myth as an allegory of the resurrection. It came to symbolize Rome, with the phoenix appearing on the coins of the late Roman Empire as an emblem of the Eternal City.

After lunch, as my taxi made its way through Dubai's midday traffic, I studied the crane-filled skyline before me and had the distinct feeling that a new phoenix had ascended.

3
Florence

Firenze

Florentia

"The god who created the hills around Florence was an artist. No! He was a jeweler, engraver, sculptor, bronze founder and painter. He was a Florentine."

—Anatole France

I always feel a rush of joy when I approach Florence. On this occasion, in the late afternoon, as the city lay tinged in violet light, my flight was on final descent into the Amerigo Vespucci Airport. As I've mentioned earlier, in 1995, after my husband's death, I went to school in Florence for most of a year. Two successive summer sessions followed, with frequent visits in-between. And, here I was again, joyous at returning to Tuscany for still another summer-school session.

After clearing Customs and Immigration, I spotted my Irish friend, Fiona, waving animatedly. "Welcome to Italy!" she said in her melodious Irish brogue after we embraced.

"It's great to be back."

"You keep succumbing to Italy's fatal charm," Fiona teased with the smile of one who has herself succumbed. Born and raised in Dublin and educated in Scotland, she came to Florence for post-graduate work in the 1970s and never left. She was now the librarian for the university where I had enrolled for summer sessions.

"I suffer from the famous Florence affliction: Duomo Fever," I said, as I wondered to myself, *Why* does *this town so captivate my heart?*

Before I attempted an answer, Fiona and I had to tackle my luggage, load it into her Fiat, and make our way through rush-hour traffic.

On previous visits I always stayed in a hotel, but this time I took a small furnished apartment in a rambling old house on Via della Colonna near Piazza San Marco. I wanted to cook while in Florence. I wanted to shop at the nearby Mercato di Sant'Ambrogio for *frutta* (fruit), *verdure* (vegetables), *salumi* (cold cuts), and *pane* (bread). I wanted to run an Italian household.

With much of historic Florence closed to automobiles, Fiona had to negotiate the city's few permissible driving streets, passing pastel buildings with rose-colored roofs. To our left coursed the nearly mythical River Arno, the great Tuscan waterway that Dante called an "accursed and unlucky ditch."

But this ditch has also been a boon. Rising in the hills of Monte Falterona in the Apennines and flowing through Tuscany to the Mediterranean, the Arno has for thousands of years provided the fresh water that supported agriculture, trade, transport, and defense. When Julius Caesar founded Florentia in 59 B.C., the river was navigable all the way to the Mediterranean, giving early Florentine merchants access to the sea and the world beyond, stoking its fledgling economic fortunes. By the third century, Florence enjoyed a population of more than ten thousand.

Leonardo da Vinci (1452-1519), who was born nearby, described water as "the vehicle of nature." He believed that this life-giving element was to the world what blood is to the human body. Because the Arno was no longer navigable as far as the sea, Leonardo tried to devise a canal system, but his dream was never realized.

As Fiona drove and I watched the ravishing Florentine vistas, I was struck again by the city's magnificent past. Moments before, I had landed at the airport that, like the entire New World, is named for a fifteenth-century Florentine, Amerigo Vespucci. And when Columbus set out in 1492 from Spain on his great transoceanic expedition, he took along navigational charts drawn up by Florentine cartographers.

Fiona had once told me that King Ferdinand of Spain commissioned Vespucci, whose navigational skills were already recognized, to confirm that Columbus had, indeed, found the New World. When Vespucci did so, Florentine cartographers were the first to generate maps of Columbus's discoveries.

When we reached my apartment, I discovered that in usual Fiona fashion, she had exceeded all expectations: Not only had she secured my key from the landlord, she had stocked my refrigerator with essentials and prepared a beautiful supper salad, *insalata di avocado, pomodori e mozzarella* (avocado, tomato, and mozzarella pasta salad). She laid out a tray of *crostini* (canapés) with egg and mushrooms. Red wine and *pesto*— that pungent sauce consisting of basil leaves, pine nuts, garlic, parmesan cheese and olive oil—completed our banquet.

When we sat down to supper, she asked if I'd noticed that the ingredients of the *insalata* matched the three colors of the Italian flag. I studied the white mozzarella cheese, the green avocado and basil, and the ripe red tomatoes. "How delightfully imaginative you are!" I said.

"I intended it as my small welcome for you to Italy," she said.

"Thank you, Fiona. It was a lovely gesture."

While we ate, we touched again on Italy's allure for us—and

for all the world, it seemed.

"I read that more than ten million visitors come to Florence each year," I said. "What do you suppose draws them?"

Fiona said that for the Irish like herself, it was Italy's "sensuality that appeals to the Northern Europeans' restrictive mores," its "spirituality and magnificent terrain." And then, of course, there's its sunshine.

"Why do *you* keep coming back?" she asked.

"Like for you, it has something to do with the joy it brings my senses and the way it stimulates my mind." I recalled the legions before me who'd been drawn to this ancient city. From the nineteenth-century Anglo-American tradition alone came such giants as Hawthorne, Thackeray, and George Eliot. Henry James, another Florence aficionado, referred to this Renaissance town as "the very sweetest among cities."

"I'm sure you've read that more than half of the world's great western art resides in Italy, and half of that is situated in Florence," Fiona said.

"Yes, and a big chunk of that art is housed in the Uffizi Gallery." As we gathered up the supper dishes, Fiona mentioned that lately she'd been using the Uffizi's policy of granting admissions by appointment. "You must try it," she urged. That was music to my ears. I recalled once, years before, waiting in line for four hours.

Since the weather was warm, we decided after dinner to partake of the city's favorite evening pastime, the *passeggiata* (stroll), when Florentines promenade, show themselves, look good (*fare bella figura*) around the main piazzas.

We strolled west in the direction of the Piazza San Marco, passing the much-honored social monument, *Spedale Degli Innocenti* (the Hospital of Innocents), Europe's first orphanage.

After its founding early in the fifteenth century, unwanted babies could be abandoned in a basin near the facility's front portico. In 1660, to provide mothers wishing to give up their children with anonymity, the basin was replaced with a rotating stone wheel upon which unwanted infants could be placed. Mothers could then ring a bell that caused the stone to turn, thus delivering their newborns into caring hands.

Fiona reminded me that the *Spedale*'s arcaded loggia was designed by none other than Filippo Brunelleschi [1377-1446], the father of Renaissance architecture. "He liked the purity and simplicity of Classical Roman buildings," she said, "and incorporated that design into the orphanage, his first true Renaissance work."

I told her that I'd read that Italy now has Europe's lowest birthrate, which rather astonished me, given the deeply Catholic tradition of this country.

"Yes, Italians almost universally defy the Vatican's teachings on contraception. Only about twenty-three percent of Italians attend mass once a month. And only about three-quarters of all cohabiting couples are married. A lot of Italians think the Vatican is out of touch with the realities of today's world. But getting back to adoption—babies in Italy are in such short supply that Italians who want to adopt often have to go through agencies in Latin America or other faraway places."

Before leaving the *Spedale*, I said hello to my favorite part of its exterior: Andrea della Robbia's glazed terra cotta rondels depicting infants cocooned in swaddling clothes.

We now headed for the Piazza San Marco, home to the University of Florence, and found it pulsating with student life.

For me, this piazza's key attraction is the Museum of San Marco, a tribute to the fifteenth-century painter, Fra Giovanni da Fiesole [1395-1455], commonly known as Fra Angelico

("Reverend Angel"). As a Dominican friar in the San Marco religious community, he painted many of his best-known frescoes, including *The Annunciation* (1438-45), which I first saw years before, hanging in unforgettable splendor in one of the Museum's corridors. It is thought to have been commissioned by Cosimo de'Medici, one of the early Florentine art patrons.

As we wandered across the piazza, Fiona asked if I'd seen the other *Annunciation* by Fra Angelico, the one officially known as the *Annunciation and Scenes from the Life of the Virgin* (1432-33), in Cortona, a nearby Tuscan town.

I recalled years ago going to Cortona on a university field trip with Professor Raffanelli, who referred to the Cortona picture as a more ecstatic portrayal of Gabriel's announcement to the Virgin that she was to give birth to the son of God. I remembered, too, in that same painting but off to the side, Fra Angelico's moving representation of Adam and Eve weeping as they were expelled from the Garden of Eden.

I asked Fiona if there was evidence that Fra Angelico embraced the progressive leanings of the early Renaissance.

"Yes, his art shows a wonderful humanity," she said. "An understanding of perspective, a sense of geometry and proportion, and light that's reminiscent, the art historians say, of his contemporary, Masaccio (1401-28), who's considered the founder of Renaissance painting."

"Didn't Pope John Paul II beatify him?" I asked.

"Yes, his life was one of total devotion and asceticism. He liked to say that he who portrays the acts of Christ should strive to be like Christ. He served the poor. He never tried to rise above his station in life, that of a humble Dominican, and he painted only after making an impassioned prayer."

I wondered if Girolamo Savonarola, the religious reformer and one-time prior of San Marco, and Fra Angelico had known each other.

"No," Fiona said, "Savonarola arrived at San Marco about thirty years after Fra Angelico died."

We left the lively student ambience, turning south toward the Piazza del Duomo, home of the Duomo [Florence's landmark cathedral that seats twenty thousand], Giotto's Tower [Campanile] and the Baptistery. Fiona mentioned that Fra Angelico's contemporary and fellow painter, Fra Filippo Lippi [c.1406-69] had been an orphan, not at the *Spedale degli Innocenti*, but with the Carmelites of Florence.

"In his teens," she said, "Filippo Lippi was pressured to become a Carmelite, but chastity and frugality proved not to be his calling. After much personal turmoil, he fell in love with a nun; both were eventually released from their vows and permitted to marry. Their son became the painter Filippino Lippi [c.1457-1504]."

"Could this kind of 'freeing from vows' have happened before the Renaissance?" I asked.

"Yes, it could have happened and *did* happen."

"How so?"

"It would have been a canonical process involving their religious superiors, although I suspect the secular spirit of the Renaissance facilitated the granting of certain religious freedoms, too."

When we reached the Piazza del Duomo, my eyes locked onto the Duomo proper, the formidable pink, green, and white Tuscan marble edifice that eclipses everything else in this compact town of about four hundred thousand. Fiona reminded me that the Duomo is the fourth largest church in the world [after St. Peter's Rome, St. Paul's London, and the Duomo in Milan].

I remembered the decree by which Arnolfo di Cambio was commissioned to construct the Duomo in 1296. The Florentine city fathers wanted to replace the old church of Santa Reparata with a structure that would surpass in size and glory anything that had been created in the golden ages of Greece or Rome. Whether the Duomo exceeds in splendor such masterpieces as the Parthenon [Greece] or Pantheon [Rome] is debatable, but with subsequent architectural additions by Giotto and Brunelleschi, the Duomo's grandeur definitely evokes wonder.

Next to the Duomo ascends Giotto's Tower, and to the right, the Baptistery, an octagonal building dating from the first century.

The Baptistery's most celebrated features are its three sets of bronze doors with relief sculptures depicting biblical scenes. The most sought out are the East Doors [facing the cathedral], designed by Lorenzo Ghiberti [1378-1455] and commissioned in 1401 to commemorate Florence's deliverance from the plague. These sculptures portray Old Testament stories such as the Creation of Adam and Eve, Noah's Ark, and Cain and Abel. When Michelangelo first saw them, he called them the "Gate of Paradise."

In spite of the growing darkness, the *passeggianti* still swarmed the piazza, especially around Ghiberti's East Doors. Fiona, who remembered the square from before the 1988 ban on traffic, rejoiced: "This piazza has become a walker's dream!"

As we strolled I was amazed at how often we saw the Medici coat of arms: six red balls on a gold backdrop. Endless debates still ensue about what they symbolize. Commonly touted theories: They signify medicinal pills, recalling the family's origin as physicians; they denote coins in memory of the Medicis' banking acumen; or they represent the six-times-dented shield of Averado, the brave eighth-century Tuscan giant killer, from whom the Medicis might have descended.

Since Fiona had to be at the university early the next morning, the start of summer term, we cut short our meanderings and headed directly for her apartment, crossing the Piazza della Repubblica, once the ancient Roman forum, and now an elegant café-lined square honoring Florence as capital of the one-time Kingdom of Italy (1865-1871). We next navigated Via Tornabuoni and from there hopscotched toward Piazza Santa Maria Novella and Fiona's home.

As we passed the piazza, Fiona and I remembered attending together a candlelight memorial mass here at Santa Maria Novella, in memory of the slain Yitzhak Rabin (1922-1995), prime minister of Israel. It was snowing, an unusual, but magical sight in this Mediterranean city, and a solemn, but treasured evening.

We said goodnight at Fiona's doorstep, knowing that tomorrow our paths would cross again at school.

As I retraced my steps along still-bustling streets, I was acutely aware of the city's history: After its founding in 59 B.C., Florentia's colonizers, retired Roman war veterans, farmed the surrounding countryside, introducing vineyards and olive groves. Instead of building arsenals for war, these retirees constructed theaters, thermal baths, country houses, and gardens.

After Rome fell in A.D. 476, barbarian tribes invaded and Florentia's fortunes plummeted. They were not rekindled until Charlemagne (742-814) restored order, uniting Western Europe for the first time since the fall of Rome. Over time, thinkers revived the humanistic values of ancient Greece and Rome in which man, not God, was believed to be the center of the universe. These changes in values fueled the Renaissance (1300-1600), a time of economic, political, and cultural fervor that marked the transition from medievalism to early-modern Europe.

Florentia's early economic boom sprang from its cloth industry. Florence imported wool from England and Spain, imported dyes from the East, and with these raw materials fabricated textiles that all of Europe came to covet. This industry employed more than thirty thousand workers. Its owners belonged to the Arte della Lana, the top trade guild, which in time became a political entity and helped Florence evolve into a free republic in which large numbers of citizens could take part. To this day, Tuscan textiles find their way into the world's most discerning fashion houses.

Commercial success during the early Renaissance helped such families as the Bardi, Peruzzi, and Medici grow to prominence, eventually gaining renown through banking. By the late 1200s their banks were transacting business for the papacy and the kingdom of Naples, with branches all over Europe.

Prominent Florentine banking families also began to dominate the city's social and political life, funding much of the art that eventually gave Florence its international acclaim. But they were not the city's only benefactors. Lesser guilds, churches, and the city government also acquired the means to commission important public and private art, thus making Florence a magnet for the leading artists of the time.

As the Renaissance advanced, the Medicis gained ascendancy, holding power almost continuously from 1434 to 1743. Key Medici names: Giovanni di Bicci (1360-1429), the banker and founder of the Medici dynasty; his son Cosimo il Vecchio (1389-1464), who multiplied the family's fortunes and became a serious patron of the arts; and Lorenzo de'Medici *(Il Magnifico)* (1449-1492), statesman, poet, and humanist—who became the uncrowned head of state of Florence during its golden years.

Not only was Lorenzo an astute diplomat and politician, influencing the Republic of Florence by placing his surrogates on the city council, he also was an enthusiastic supporter of art and literature. In fact, he became a creative entity in his own right, with poetry his particular passion.

Lorenzo brought into his court the most brilliant artists and thinkers of his day, among them, Leonardo da Vinci, Donatello, Sandro Botticelli, Domenico Ghirlandaio, Andrea del Verrocchio, and Michelangelo Buonarroti.

Early on, Lorenzo recognized Michelangelo's unique talents, inviting the young apprentice to become a student at the Medici sculpture garden, a school of the arts, and to live in the Palazzo Medici as one of his sons, even dining at his table. Until Lorenzo's death four years later, Michelangelo thrived in that environment. After he became a great sculptor, Michelangelo reflected on his artistic gifts, which he cultivated for a time under the aegis of *Il Magnifico*: "I saw the angel in the marble and carved until I set him free."

The American university where I was to attend summer school was one of several U.S. institutions of higher learning with satellite campuses in Florence. It operated from a Renaissance palazzo modeled after the city's stately Medici and Pitti Palaces. Bold-bossed and rusticated stonework, austere facades, semicircular window arches, and strict proportions were among the hallmarks of what was once a prestigious urban residence. Each time I saw it, I couldn't help but think of the Residenz in Munich, which I describe in Chapter One.

The dean was Father Martini, an elderly Jesuit who had run the campus for twenty-eight years. The coming academic year would be his last in Florence; a successor had already been named. At age seventy-seven, with teaching still a joy, Father Martini decided to step back into the classroom one last time to teach a course titled, "Renaissance Writers: Dante [1265-1321], Petrarch [1304-1374], and Boccaccio [1313-1375]." I had never spent much time studying Italy's Renaissance literary tradition. This was my chance, and with Father Martini at the podium I couldn't resist.

Our class consisted of eighteen students, mainly American women from West Coast universities, and me, closer in age to Father Martini than to my classmates.

Father Martini opened his lecture by describing the *Divine Comedy* as an allegorical poem that grew out of Dante Alighieri's own political travails: While exiled from Florence by the Black Guelfs, a political faction, Dante devised the *Divine Comedy* as a way to show his contempt for the pettiness that he believed most men displayed.

"Dante is also remembered," Father Martini told us, "for breaking with tradition, which scorned the Tuscan vernacular for literary works and made it the literary standard for the Italian language." (Until 1300, Latin had been the Italian peninsula's sole literary language.)

Having read about Thomas Mann's struggle with exile, I was moved to read that Dante suffered from banishment as well. For him it was a kind of death.

Dante died in exile in Ravenna, and Father Martini arranged for us to make a day trip to this ancient city near the Adriatic to view Dante's tomb. He explained how Florence later regretted expelling him.

By 1829 Florentine city fathers had grown so determined to bring Dante home that they constructed an elaborate tomb for him in the Franciscan basilica of Santa Croce, (built c.1294), where such notables as Michelangelo and Galileo rest. "But the tomb has remained empty and Dante continues to lie in Ravenna, far from the place where he hoped to find peace," Father Martini explained.

Toward the end of his lectures, Father Martini walked with us to Santa Croce to view the stately but empty tomb. En route we stopped at the Casa di Dante (Dante's House) on Via Santa Margherita, a museum that pays tribute to the poet's life.

The literary work that most consumed the class was Boccaccio's *The Decameron,* perhaps because of the story's backdrop: the Black Death. In a time of heightened awareness of HIV and other pandemics, the students were mesmerized by the bubonic plague-induced crisis that struck Europe around 1347-1351 and killed between one-third to two-thirds of the Continent's population. The Black Death took a particularly lethal toll on Florence.

The plague's typical onset was swelling in the groin and armpit, often the size of eggs or apples.

Crystal, a nursing student from Colorado, told our class that from a research project on the Black Death she had learned the pandemic included the Middle East, India, and China. "It's believed to have been caused by the bacterium *Yersinia pestis,* and spread by fleas on animals like black rats." She informed us that the disease probably started in the steppes of Asia and was brought west by traders and Mongol armies along the Silk Road. Europeans got their first exposure via trading ports such as Genoa and Venice.

"Why was it called the *Black* Death?" Ashley asked.

Father Martini explained that originally people thought the name was based on a symptom called *acral necrosis,* in which the sufferer's skin undergoes a subdermal hemorrhage, causing it to darken. Now researchers think the term might only reflect the grim nature of the illness.

Joshua asked if other contemporary literary works discussed the Black Death.

"Chaucer wrote about it in *The Canterbury Tales* and William Langland addressed it in *Piers Plowman,*" Father Martini said. "Three centuries later the diarist Samuel Pepys left an unparalleled portrait of the London plague of 1665." After reflecting for a moment, he added, "If you want to see a movie classic on the subject, I suggest that when you get back home you rent the 1957 Ingmar Bergman film *The Seventh Seal.*"

"Oh, I've seen that," chimed Daniel, a normally quiet student in the back of the class. "A knight comes back from the Crusades and finds his homeland pillaged by the plague. He realizes that Death has come for him, too, and to buy time he challenges Death to a game of chess—anything to let him reach his home after an absence of ten years. That's all I'm gonna say. I don't want to give the end away."

"That was good, Daniel. Thank you," Father Martini said, telling us in the eyes of some, the church failed miserably in bringing comfort as the epidemic rampaged. "Where is God's mercy?" people cried as thousands around them died. This seeming abandonment by God contributed to the church's decline for a time. We learned that the fourteenth-century outbreak of the Black Death in and around Florence also caused the economy to falter and patronage for the visual arts to decline.

"As if to compensate for these losses," Father Martini lectured, "the great Italian literary tradition sprang to life, with men of letters such as those we're looking at this summer."

After this short digression, Father Martini continued his commentary on *The Decameron.* Seven young women and three young men decide to escape plague-infested Florence for two weeks and flee to a country house where they believe they will be safe from infection. To amuse themselves, each participant tells a story for five nights of each week spent at the house. In all, the escapees told a hundred stories, ranging in subject matter from the erotic to the tragic.

After weaving our way through many of *The Decameron's* tales, some happy, some sad, and discussing the overall nature of tragedy, be it bubonic plague or AIDS, a student from Oklahoma asked, "In a just world, it seems that the innocent should prosper and the wicked suffer, as *Psalms* 37 suggests.

What is your take on why God allows bad things to happen to good people?"

Clearly, Father Martini had been asked this question before. With ease he spoke about the need for faith in a time like this.

"We don't have all the facts about suffering," he said, adding that pain can also serve a higher good. "God is in control of the universe no matter how it looks to the casual observer." Aware that several students in the class shared his faith, he reminded them to "seek the comfort that only God can bestow in the wake of tragedy."

I liked my apartment on Via della Colonna, although it had seen better days. The gas stove ignited only after multiple attempts. The washer worked only if I disconnected the refrigerator. And the laundry dried only if I hung it across chairs and doors. (There was no dryer or clothesline.) But the flat's proximity to the Mercato di Sant'Ambrogio made up for its deficiencies. At the Mercato, *io facevo la spesa* (I went shopping for food). Though in Florence to study art and culture, I also wanted to grow in my appreciation for the traditional bond between Italy's land and the people it nourished.

Mercato di Sant'Ambrogio's outdoor section, under a covered portico, bustled with stalls displaying tomatoes, eggplants, zucchinis, peaches, figs, ropes of garlic, or whatever was in season. Nearby were stalls selling fresh herbs, especially basil, the key aromatic plant for Italian cooking. Fresh flowers, housewares, and clothing stands completed this scene of plenty.

Indoors, under a central covered space and displayed in glass cases, fish, meat, cheese and bread lay arranged as if in a painted still-life. I liked watching spirited Florentine housewives bargain with vendors who seduced them with buoyant cries of "*assaggi*" (taste it) or "*provi*" (try it).

"*No, grazie. Ne ho abbastanza,*" I'd often heard in response. (No, thank you, I have enough).

The sight of Tuscan bread *(pane toscano)*, usually in the form of an oval golden loaf, always reminded me that it comes without salt, but for a reason: Before the unification of Italy in 1870, when Italy was a series of cantankerous city-states, Florence acquired its salt from the neighboring sea-bound city-state of Pisa. Legend says that Florentines grew so weary of finding the *gabelliere*, the Pisan salt-tax collector, knocking at their door that they decided to fight back by baking their bread without salt.

My goal on this shopping day was to buy the ingredients for ribollita, Tuscany's most famous soup, sometimes called a "peasant" dish.

For centuries many on the Italian peninsula knew hardship and privation: droughts, storms, erratic seas, wars, foreign domination, and diseases. A cooking teacher of mine once remarked that the basic ingredients found in age-old dishes such as ribollita honor those who suffered and endured. This simple soup made from leftovers must once have constituted the only meal of the day for many poor Tuscans.

The ingredients of my favorite ribollita recipe:
(from *Soups*, edited by Felicity Forster; interpreted by my Florence friends)

> 3 tablespoons olive oil
> 2 onions, chopped
> 2 carrots, sliced
> 4 garlic cloves, crushed
> 2 celery stalks, thinly sliced
> 1 fennel bulb, trimmed and chopped
> 1 pound *cavolo nero* (black cabbage), shredded
> 2 large zucchini, thinly sliced

14-ounce can chopped tomatoes
2 tablespoons homemade or store-bought pesto
3-3/4 cups vegetable stock
14-ounce can navy or pinto beans, drained
Salt and ground pepper
At the end:
1 tablespoon extra virgin olive oil,
    plus extra for drizzling.
6-8 slices crusty white bread
Parmesan cheese shavings

In spite of my taste for Tuscany's simple and unrefined peasant dishes, Florentines take rightful pride in their sumptuous culinary tradition, one that accommodated the aristocracy and prosperous merchant class.

After Catherine de'Medici married Henry II of France in 1535, she imported to France a coterie of Tuscan chefs who brought along elegant indigenous recipes. After pioneering culinary affectations such as introducing the fork to the French(!) and serving pastries out of which live pigeons flew, Catherine became known as "the mother of French cuisine."

❀

Professor Eleanora Raffanelli, my art history teacher from years before, taught a course titled "Excursions into the Baroque," a survey of the seventeenth-century period that defied classical rules by expressing emotion and human drama in painting, sculpture, architecture, literature, dance, and music. It was an art movement that relished detail such as in ornamentation and embellishment. "The Baroque should evoke a sense of awe," Raffanelli said. In her class that summer, we addressed the Baroque in painting.

I liked best the days she took us to the Giorgio Vasari-designed Galleria degli Uffizi, once intended as the offices (*uffizi*) for the new Tuscan administration of Duke Cosimo I de'Medici (1519-74). She explained that Duke Cosimo I had a despotic streak and thought nothing of killing dissidents and rivals. In consequence, he amassed a great many enemies. So, to reduce his need for travel and thus his exposure to assassination attempts, he decided in the 1550s to consolidate his many far-flung judicial and administrative offices under one roof. In 1559 he hired Giorgio Vasari, Tuscan architect, painter, and writer, to design and build a modern bureaucratic center adjacent to what was then Duke Cosimo's residence, Palazzo della Signoria, also called Palazzo Vecchio.

Vasari designed this new complex in the late-Renaissance style. Completed in 1556, it consists of two long parallel wings connected at one end, shaped like a horseshoe. A narrow interior courtyard spills toward the river, and an almost continuous wall of glass spans the top floor, capturing the brilliant light typical of Florence. An airy loggia overlooks the Arno.

In 1560 Duke Cosimo and his family moved across the River Arno to the newly refurbished Pitti Palace. In 1565, to make his new bureaucratic center readily accessible but spare the Medicis the need to step into the street, he commissioned Vasari to construct the so-called Vasari Corridor, an elevated private walkway that courses from the Palazzo Vecchio, via the Uffizi and the Ponte Vecchio, to the Pitti Palace. Fine art lines this corridor and can be seen on a guided tour that lasts about three hours.

Cosimo I died in 1574, at the age of 55. His son and heir, Grand-duke Francesco I de'Medici (1541-1587), during a benevolent moment, sanctioned the use of the well-lighted top floor of the Uffizi to display some of his family's art treasures. Thus was born in 1581 the Galleria, today believed to be the oldest art gallery in the western world, housing two singular collections: The Galleria degli Uffizi, intimately associated with the Renaissance, mainly showcases masterpieces dating from the thirteenth to the nineteenth century. The Gabinetto Disegni e Stampe contains nearly one hundred twenty thousand drawings and prints, a collection begun in the mid-sixteenth century and still expanding today. In addition, the Uffizi features research and conservation institutes that accommodate scholars from all over the world.

An addendum to this tale: The last ruling Medici, Anna Maria Luisa de'Medici (1667-1743) actually bestowed on Florence her incalculable artistic legacy.

Even the stroll to the Uffizi was a joy: Upon leaving the university on Via Tornabuoni, we zigzagged through narrow cobblestoned lanes that gave way to broader streets until we reached Piazza della Signoria, the heart of Florentine politics since the fourteenth century. In the eyes of some, this piazza is an open-air museum. Among its features are: Donatello's fifteenth-century Marzocco (heraldic lion), Michelangelo's statue of David (a copy—the original resides in the Accademia of Florence), Cellini's bronze statue of Perseus, and Ammannati's Neptune Fountain.

I love this piazza and come to it often for coffee at Caffé Rivoire, opposite the Palazzo Vecchio, built from 1298-1302 as the seat of local government. But on this day I couldn't be waylaid by its splendor. We were off to see two of the Uffizi's prime examples of the Baroque, by Caravaggio (1573-1610).

In the painting titled *The Young Bacchus,* the wine god enjoys his cup of bliss. Professor Raffanelli called attention to the painting's sexual innuendos—the god's nearly naked torso, flushed face, and heavy eyelids.

After looking awhile, Melissa from Oregon asked, "What are we to make of the wine god's seductive offering of wine, as if to us, and his sleepy eye-contact with us viewers?"

"It might well be a summons for more than just a drink."

At this, Zachary asked, "What's that plate of decaying fruit in front of the wine god supposed to mean? That's hardly summoning."

"Caravaggio used symbols to make statements," our teacher said. "In this case he's commenting on the impermanence of life. The body that is today sensual and prime, in time will wither and die."

Next Professor Raffanelli turned to Caravaggio's *The Sacrifice of Isaac* (1603), quoting to us from *Genesis* 22:1-12, in which God tests Abraham.

The professor then pointed out how skillfully Caravaggio portrayed Abraham's anguish in this painting. Before leaving the museum, we moved on to still another example of the Baroque: Caravaggio's *Head of Medusa*, an image that my classmates found "gross." For extra credit, Professor Raffanelli encouraged us to visit the Pitti Palace on our own to view Pietro da Cortona's Baroque ceilings.

Before leaving, we passed Botticelli's famous *The Birth of Venus* (1484-86). As we paused before the image of Venus borne up by a large shell, I saw one of my classmates, Nicole from Arizona, point and say to Ashley next to her, "That's so fucking *beautiful!*"

I must have looked surprised, since Professor Raffanelli later whispered in my ear: "Nowadays, *fucking* is just an intensifier. It means *very.*"

My long road to becoming educated.

❀

On the following Saturday I took up Professor Raffanelli's suggestion to visit the Pitti Palace in the Oltrarno, a district south of the River Arno. For centuries it was considered a lesser neighborhood: more rural and blue-collar, full of artisans with modest houses. People who couldn't afford to live in the heart of the city, the north bank, migrated to Oltrarno.

In 1457, Luca Pitti, an ambitious banker, eager to enhance his standing in Florence society, decided to try to build a palace even grander than the Medicis'. He chose the Oltrarno as his site and hired Filippo Brunelleschi as his architect, with Luca Fancelli as his assistant. Every detail of the Pitti Palace was meant to surpass the north bank's Palazzo Medici; even the windows and doors had to be larger. By 1465 Luca Pitti had fallen victim to his vanity. Building costs had bankrupted him; construction ceased.

Ironically, in 1549, Eleanora of Toledo, the wife of Cosimo I de'Medici, bought the long-abandoned Pitti Palace, tripled its size, and established it as the family's ducal palace, which became their power base for hundreds of years.

Once the Medicis made Oltrarno acceptable, other prominent Florentine families followed. The palace remained the principal Medici residence until the last male heir died in 1737. Then it passed to other royal houses until 1919, when Vittorio Emanuele III, King of Italy from 1900-1946, officially presented it to the nation.

Since then it has been home to a series of princely galleries displaying Medici art collected over five centuries: Galleria Palatina (Palatine Gallery), Galleria d'Arte Moderna (Modern Art Gallery), the Museo degli Argenti (Silver Museum), Appartamenti Monumentali (State Apartments), Galleria del Costume (Costume Gallery), and the Museo delle Carrozze that houses state carriages and sedan chairs.

I've always liked the decorative arts, and the Pitti Palace contains a breathtaking collection of delicately wrought objects made from precious metals, amber, ivory, lapis lazuli, rock crystal, and porcelain. *Che meraviglia!* Among my favorites are the rock crystal pieces—a heron-shaped vase mounted in gold, enamel, and precious stones. It was crafted in the Milanese workshop of the Saracchi family, who had a penchant for bird-shaped receptacles and bizarre imagery. Pieces like this one reminded me of others I'd seen in the Treasury of the Munich Residenz and the Green Vault in Dresden.

When I asked Professor Raffanelli about collecting as an art form, she said that it would be wrong to suggest that collecting *per se* began with the Renaissance. Cathedral treasuries had long been around, she said, but collecting for secular display came into play around 1500, during the Italian Renaissance. Decades later, as the Renaissance moved north to Germany, the Netherlands and France, the aristocracy and rich merchant class of those lands also embraced collecting as an art form. Collecting requires a certain level of education and means, which these social classes had.

After touring the Pitti Palace, I ventured into the highly stylized Boboli Gardens, built from 1549-1579 and opened to the public in 1766. This tract of land is a mass of terraces, fountains, grottoes, and collections of Roman, Renaissance, and Baroque sculpture—a comment on aristocratic leisure through the last five centuries. My guidebook pointed me to the most popular sculpture in the garden, the *Bacchus Fountain*, which is a copy of the original by Valerio Cioli. The statue depicts a portly naked dwarf (he was Cosimo I's court dwarf) astride a turtle in the role of Bacchus, whose Caravaggian incarnation I'd just seen at the Uffizi some days before.

From here it was easy to access the grounds around Fort Belvedere, built in 1590 to guard Florence against attacks by political opponents. Later it became a retreat for the Medici grand dukes.

As I sat on Fort Belvedere's lawns taking in the view, I remembered first coming to this spot in 1995 to do battle with irregular Italian verbs. Then and now, the Duomo, almost palpable at eye level, overpowered me.

After an hour or so of consuming this visual banquet, I left to meet Fiona in front of Casa Guidi, the Oltrarno home (1847-1861) of the celebrated English poets Elizabeth Barrett and Robert Browning. I hurried down the Boboli Garden hillside, passed the Kaffeehaus and Ganymede Fountain, passed through the Pitti Palace exit and across the Piazza de Pitti to the Casa Guidi.

Fiona was nowhere in sight. Although it was Saturday, I knew she had to stop at the university to help a student with a research project. While I waited, I read the commemorative tablet placed by the city of Florence on Casa Guidi. Translated from the Italian, it reads:

> *Here wrote and died*
> *Elizabeth Barrett Browning*
> *Who in her woman's heart had a poet's spirit*
> *And whose poems forged a golden ring*
> *Between Italy and England*
> *Grateful Florence*
> *Sets this memorial*
> *1861*

In the early 1840s, Robert Browning (1812-1889), then still a largely unknown poet and playwright, came across a book of poetry by the internationally famous Elizabeth Barrett (1806-1861). He was so impressed with her work that he wrote her a fan letter: "I love your verses with all my heart, dear Miss Barrett ... and I love you too."

Elizabeth was six years older than her admirer, a semi-invalid, a spinster, and jealously guarded by her widower-father. Still, Elizabeth responded favorably to Robert's overture. Correspondence followed. In May of 1845, in her father's home on Wimpole Street in London, Robert Browning called on her for the first time. Chemistry ignited. In spite of her father's strenuous disapproval, the two lovers eloped to Italy where they feasted on sunshine and freedom.

After spending their first winter in Pisa, they moved to Florence, where they settled into Casa Guidi among "six beautiful rooms and a kitchen, three of them quite palace rooms and opening on a terrace," Elizabeth wrote to a friend. In this setting, her health improved, and in 1849 she bore a son, Robert Wiedemann "Pen" Barrett Browning, their only child.

In Florence, Elizabeth home-schooled Pen, became a social advocate and humanitarian, and wrote prodigiously. Robert absorbed the expanding energies of the Renaissance and later incorporated them into his writings. He became a master of the dramatic monologue, which let him voice his thoughts through fictional characters.

Elizabeth's biographers say that she was always frail, and in June 1861 she caught a cold that aggravated her lifelong battle with lung disease. Her doctor tried every remedy available, but she finally succumbed at Casa Guidi on June 29, 1861.

Over the years Elizabeth had become such a beloved presence in Florence that on the day of her funeral the shops on their street closed while newspapers mournfully proclaimed her death. She was buried in the English Cemetery of Florence on July 1. (When I visited her final resting place in July 2011, I found an elaborate two-tiered, white marble tomb adorned with fresh flowers.)

Soon after her death, Robert transcribed into Elizabeth's Bible a passage from Dante: "Thus I believe, thus I affirm, thus I am certain it is, that from this life I shall pass to another better, there, where that lady lives of whom my soul was enamoured."

Within days of her funeral, Minister Ubaldino Peruzzi, a distinguished Italian politician, paid a visit to Browning, saying that "the Italians all were anxious" that he not leave Florence and that "Pen might continue to be 'a Tuscan.'"

However, Robert Browning and his young son did leave. Robert felt a need to break with the past. They moved north, living mainly in England, with France their preferred holiday destination. Pen attended Christ Church in Oxford, but failed his final exams. He left the university in 1870 to study sculpture and painting. As a widower, Robert became serious about writing; in time he gained more literary fame than his late wife, who'd been the light of his life. Other women danced around the periphery of his world, but none possessed the key that would unlock his heart again.

In 1879 Robert and Pen moved to Venice, making their home in Palazzo Rezzonico. There Pen eventually married. In 1889 Robert developed bronchitis and heart failure, and died on December 12. Although he wanted to be buried with Elizabeth, the small English cemetery in Florence was then closed to further burials; he rests in London's Westminster Abbey.

"*Ciao*, Rose Marie!"

I spun around and saw Fiona approaching on Via Maggio. "*Come va?*" I responded.

"*Non c'e male, e tu?*"

"*Bene, molto bene, grazie.*"

Fiona apologized for her half-hour delay, and we headed just a few blocks away from Casa Guidi to Santo Spirito, our chief destination for the day. The great sculptor Gian Lorenzo Bernini (1598-1680) described Santo Spirito as "the most beautiful church in the world."

As we walked I asked Fiona the question I'd been storing up for days: What became of all the art and artifacts of Florence when World War II broke out? Some of the art had found its way into hiding throughout the Tuscan countryside, she replied, while other pieces fell into Nazi hands. Toward the end of the war, as the Nazis retreated north, truckloads of plunder went to depots in northern Italy. When the Germans surrendered on May 2, 1945, they also surrendered what they had stolen.

"An interesting World War II footnote," she added, "is that one of the American officers assigned to escort the looted treasures back to Florence was none other than Frederick Hartt." The preeminent American art historian of the Italian Renaissance is known especially for *Art: A History of Painting, Sculpture, and Architecture*.

I asked how the U.S. Army used this young man's talents.

"Primarily as an interpreter of photographs," Fiona said. "Later he received the Bronze Star for his part in the repatriation of stolen art."

Frederick Hartt came to Florence's rescue again during November 1966 when the River Arno's flood nearly annihilated more than seven hundred years of the town's history. After arriving in Florence to inspect the devastation, Hartt told a group of journalists that Athens and Florence have a particularly important place in the history of human civilization. Having done all he could to help Florence on site, he returned to the United States to marshal aid: human and monetary.

Entering Santo Spirito, I found it light, spacious, with elegant archways and thirty-eight semicircular side chapels. We'd both been here before, but Fiona wanted me to take a closer look at side chapel #11 which features *Madonna with Child and Saints* (1490-1493), considered one of Filippino Lippi's most important works.

The garments in the painting ripple with vibrant colors, especially red. The architectural elements, with their delicate gold-relief decorations, display truly fine details. The landscape in the background reminded me of Lippi's contemporary, Leonardo da Vinci, whose art he had surely studied. I especially liked how baby Jesus gambols in the foreground.

Fiona and I then strolled to an open-air trattoria in the Piazza di Santo Spirito, where the afternoon sun lulled us. Fiona ordered *tortino alla Toscana* (baby artichoke omelette) and I *merluzzo con verdure* (cod with vegetables). We closed our meal with an espresso and *lamponi con panna* (raspberries with cream).

Late one afternoon just before summer school finals, I decided to try to catch Father Martini in his office to say goodbye. Since I would not be taking exams, I planned to leave Florence early the next morning for Málaga, Spain. There I would join friends to explore "Al-Andalus" or Andalusia: the vigorous civilization of early medieval Europe and a place where Jews, Muslims, and Christians worked in harmony and prosperity, pooling resources of language, art, science, scholarship, and commerce.

Predictably, the old priest's office door was ajar; faculty and students made good use of this open-door policy. "Do you have a minute?" was how an encounter usually began. He had many minutes; that was his job. A priest foregoes family and home to serve his flock. It had been this white-haired man's lifelong joy to work with youth. I sometimes sensed his regret that his Florentine years were coming to a close, that his life was ebbing, but he would never let on. He believed in the natural progression of life: We are born, we live, we die. He believed fervently in the *paradiso* that awaited him.

I once asked a younger Jesuit acquaintance, who served as rector of his community, how the older priests in his population accepted the inevitable coming of the end. I presumed that because of their training and faith, the younger priest would say, "Gracefully, stoically, or with anticipation." Instead, he said,

"Many of them are scared to death."

"Hello, Father, do you have a minute?" I asked as I peeked in his door.

"Come in, Rose Marie," he answered.

When I told him I was leaving in the morning, he said, "It was good to have you, Rose Marie. You seem to have become a fixture here in Florence."

"Yes, sort of like the guest who came for dinner and never left. Thank you for having me again."

I asked Father Martini if he had enjoyed his return to teaching after his years as an administrator.

"Yes, it's revitalizing . . . the world of ideas and youth. Youth and age coalesce well. Youth invigorates an old man's spirit, and perhaps an old man's spirit can still infuse youth with something of value, too."

I wondered if he ever thought about "the road not taken." Was the priesthood the only path for him? Could he have found fulfillment in other walks of life? Marriage? Children? Are there not many ways to serve God?

It was not my place to probe such matters with him. I recall reading that when a nun from a conservative religious order was asked similar questions, she said that she was thankful that she only had to make that decision once. Could she do it again? She didn't know. The spur for such a move, she believed, had come to her in a moment of grace.

After paying my respects to Father Martini, I strolled in the direction of the Ponte Vecchio, today the pedestrians-only jewelers' bridge, and since Roman times a strategic River Arno crossing. During the Middle Ages fishmongers, butchers, and leatherworkers plied their trades on this ancient structure, using the Arno as their garbage dump. But Grand Duke Ferdinando

I, offended by the ensuing stench and noise, decreed during his sixteenth-century reign that more refined enterprises replace them; hence, the evolution that led to what is now the jewelers' bridge.

On this day I wanted to buy a "fiorino d'oro" of the Republic of Florence—an Italian gold coin struck from 1252 to 1523, and once the dominant currency of Western Europe for large-scale transactions. The front of the florin coin features the symbol of Florence (the *Iris florentia*, contoured like a fleur-de-lis); and the back shows John the Baptist, patron saint of Florence. After all my Florence sojourns, I thought I finally owed myself a florin pendant.

Most shops carried them. All it took was my faithful credit card and, *eccoci!* (presto!), I was the proud owner of a beautiful new coin. Another possession to keep track of.

Midway across the bridge I studied once again the bust of Benvenuto Cellini, the most famous of all Florentine goldsmiths, after which I gazed into the Arno, with its shimmering yellow-brown water. I knew that following my Andalusia visit, I'd be feasting on the Pacific Northwest's transparent blue waters.

While for millennia the Arno has bolstered the economic fortunes of Florence, its tendency to flood has brought repeated misery. History records that in 1333, the river produced a deluge so monstrous that an early fortified version of today's Ponte Vecchio washed away. It was rebuilt in 1345 only to be battered again in 1557. The Nazi retreat during World War II brought further mayhem, but nothing compared to the devastation wrought by the November 4, 1966, overflow that destroyed everything in its path, a matter I've already touched on in reference to Frederick Hartt.

The Archives of the Opera del Duomo suffered damage to six thousand volumes/documents and fifty-five illustrated manuscripts. The Gabinetto Scientifico Letterario G. P.

Vieusseux Library said that a quarter million of its books had been damaged; the National Library Centers of Florence testified that 1,300,000 articles such as prints and maps had been destroyed. Even the venerable Uffizi's basement, storage place for thousands of Renaissance paintings, fell victim to the flood. The list of destruction goes on and on.

Still today in Florence, stories abound of *angeli del fango* (mud angels)—volunteers from around the world who risked their lives to help salvage historical treasures. Fiona acknowledged that American students were among the most determined to help in the rescue.

Was Fiona one of them? She said no, that she did not arrive in Florence until the early 1970s, but she knew many who as youths had come to clean up the disaster, even happily sleeping in railroad cars.

As I strolled from the Ponte Vecchio to the restaurant La Spada near Via Tornabuoni where I would meet Fiona, Marcella, and Paolo (friends from my earlier student days in Florence) for a farewell dinner, I saluted the Florentines' extraordinary achievements—in commerce, politics and art. What other city produced a Dante, Giotto, da Vinci or Michelangelo? I also paid homage to Tuscany in general, the Central Italian region in which Florence lies. It produced its share of geniuses, too: Petrarch, Botticelli, Galileo Galilei, Amerigo Vespucci, Luca Pacioli, and Puccini. What accounts for that kind of concentrated brilliance?

Scholars have taken up this question, suggesting that it was the Tuscan passion for study and hard work. Some have speculated that Tuscany's genius came from its multi-layered history and ensuing diversity. My sense is that all these factors played a role.

When I reached La Spada, Fiona was already waiting.

"*Carissima*," she said as we embraced.

"*Carissima mia*," I replied.

Just then Marcella and Paolo burst through the door, and after a long round of *buona seras* and *come vas*, along with hugs and kisses, we settled into our celebration in this *città meravigliosa* [wonderful city] of which I will always be a student.

4

Andalusia

Andalucía

"It is no exaggeration to say that what we presumptuously call 'Western' culture is owed in large measure to the Andalusian enlightenment."
—Christopher Hitchens,
The Nation

It was a *story* that first prompted me to travel to Andalusia:

In A.D. 750, a desperate young prince fled his home in Damascus, Syria, then the heart of Islam, in search of a safe haven. His entire family, the ruling Umayyads of the House of Islam, had just been annihilated. Some years before, the Umayyads had successfully led the Muslims from the barren deserts of Arabia to the developed cultures of the Fertile Crescent.

Successors to and descendents of Prophet Mohammed's inner circle, the Umayyads died at the hands of their rivals, the Abbasids, who then took control over the House of Islam, eventually making their capital in Baghdad.

Barely twenty and a political refugee, prince Abd al-Rahman journeyed across North Africa to a region the Muslims called the *Maghrib*, the farthest western outpost of the ever-expanding Islamic empire. Today known as Morocco, this was the ancestral home of Abd al-Rahman's mother, a member of the Berber tribe (non-Arab nomads of North Africa), that had lived between the Sahara and the Mediterranean since earliest recorded time.

Five years after the Damascus bloodbath, when Abd al-Rahman surfaced in the *Maghrib*, he found that many Berbers had already converted to Islam. These newly converted believers, often referred to as Moors (an inexact but now generally accepted term to describe primarily the Muslim Berbers and Syrian Arabs, who invaded Spain) had crossed the Straits of Gibraltar to a land the Romans called Hispania or Iberia. Arab-speakers called it "al-Andalus," the southernmost region of today's Spain. Abd al-Rahman followed them and built a new life.

In a town called Qurtuba (Córdoba) on the River Guadalquivir, he encountered a thriving Islamic colony. Although the region surrounding Córdoba had been ravaged by early occupiers—Phoenicians, Carthaginians, Greeks, Romans, and most recently the Visigoths from the north—Abd al-Rahman saw potential in the land, if only the leadership were right.

As the sole surviving heir of the Umayyads of Damascus, a Berber (through his mother), and in the minds of many an exemplar of what was best among the newly-arrived Muslim Arabs, Abd al-Rahman quickly won the support of these recent settlers. In A.D. 756, he went to war with al-Andalus' existing *emir* (Arabic for governor) and defeated him, proclaiming himself the new head of this westernmost province of the Islamic world. He came to be known as Abd al-Rahman I, sometimes simply as "the Immigrant." He created a new emirate (governorship) with Córdoba as its capital and ruled from 756 to 788. The now-resurrected branch of the Umayyads survived for nine generations to come.

Abd al-Rahman made Arabic the emirate's language of

governance, worship, and commerce. This helped maintain ties to the larger and more established Islamic world from which he imported the technology, and later the scholarship, necessary to build his emirate into an imposing polity.

Under Abd al-Rahman I's steady hand, the region transformed itself from a debilitated place into a cultural treasure, described by one enthusiastic visitor then as "the ornament of the world."

Córdoba fattened into a city of five hundred thousand inhabitants, with public works that included paved and lighted roads, bridges, running water, and irrigation facilities. The emirate imported plant life—such as cotton, citrus, figs, spinach, and watermelon. Libraries blossomed, one with six hundred thousand manuscripts. More than seven hundred mosques proliferated, along with the Great Mosque of Córdoba, also called the *Mezquita,* the most arresting expression of Islam on the Iberian Peninsula.

A guide later told me that inscriptions over academic portals in Islamic Spain often read:

The world is supported by four things only: the learning of the wise, the justice of the great, the prayers of the righteous and the valor of the brave.

At its pinnacle during the early tenth century, Córdoba became one of the world's great cultural, economic and political centers. Andalusia under the Umayyads was an open-minded and innovative society where Jews, Christians, and Muslims lived together in harmony and prosperity, pooling resources of language, art, science, scholarship, and commerce. During this time, regular contact with the advanced cultures of the Fertile Crescent continued. The translation and preservation of Greco/ Roman writings were high priorities in the learning centers of Damascus and Baghdad. These translations found their way into Córdoban libraries, filling them with artistic and scientific manuscripts otherwise unavailable in the Western world.

Hungry to connect with long-forgotten works from the classical world, northern European scholars flooded into Córdoba. A cultural flowering ensued throughout Europe, fueling the Renaissance and the eventual Age of Enlightenment.

By 929, the Golden Age initiated by Abd al-Rahman I had become so burnished that he had a proclamation read from all the mosques of al-Andalus, declaring that Abd al-Rahman III, direct descendent of the immigrant prince, was now the rightful defender of the faith, the lawful caliph of the entire Islamic world, and the religious head of all Muslims.

This irritated some rival claimants to power. Strife set in. *Fitnas* (civil wars) followed, splintering the Caliphate of Córdoba into more than two dozen *taifas* (small Arab states).

Seeing weakness in the once formidable al-Andalus, the Almoravids, radical Muslim Berber tribesmen whose seat of power lay in what is now Morocco, conquered southern Spain in 1086, only to be displaced in 1146 by the Almohads, even more radical Muslim Berber tribesmen, also from North Africa.

By the thirteenth century, al-Andalus began falling into the hands of the consolidated and powerful northern Christian kingdoms that had long nursed resentments against al-Andalus. Córdoba crumbled in 1236 and Seville in 1248. The collapse of Granada, in 1492, ended the eight hundred-year-long Islamic presence on the Iberian Peninsula, and thus in Europe.

Some say that Abd al-Rahman's Golden Age was merely a historical footnote that failed; others say it was unquestionably a success, producing a powerful fusion of commerce, scholarship, and power in a blighted place, seeding the Renaissance and Enlightenment, and bringing together Jews, Christians, and Muslims, who shared the best that each had to offer.

In spite of my exposure to Middle Eastern culture early in my adult life, an understanding of the *degree* to which Arab

88

culture influenced early-medieval Europe, and thereby Western civilization, had escaped me. Certainly, I never learned anything about it while in school; it was simply not taught. The story of medieval Spain's long flowering of art, architecture, culture, and commerce seems a sadly neglected part of Western history.

❀

Now well into the new millennium, I was met at the Málaga airport by my congenial, mustachioed guide, Sebastiano. We were to drive in his van from Málaga to Córdoba, about two hours north on Highway A-45, where I would meet my hosts and traveling companions, Tom and Barbara, old friends from my United Arab Emirates years.

On the following day, under Sebastiano's guidance, we would begin our tour of al-Andalus, starting with Córdoba, where the visionary immigrant prince sowed the first seeds of medieval Spain's Golden Age of Enlightenment. Then we would explore Seville and Granada, which also figured in medieval Spain's amazing metamorphosis.

Years before, Tom and Barbara had lived in Bahrain, where he worked with the oil industry, and they had both developed an interest in Arab culture. It was they who first told me the story of Abd al-Rahman, amplifying their tale by giving me María Rosa Menocal's *The Ornament of the World: How Muslims, Jews, and Christians Created a Culture of Tolerance in Medieval Spain*. After reading it, I knew I'd have to travel to Andalusia to see firsthand the world that Menocal described. When Tom and Barbara asked me to extend my Florence sojourn to join them in looking at medieval Spain's golden age, I jumped at the opportunity.

Hardly had Sebastiano and I pulled out of the Mediterranean port city of Málaga proper, when we saw the sunny hillsides, terraced slopes, and well-positioned vineyards of the Andalusian countryside.

"Are these the vineyards where the Málaga sweet wine comes from?" I asked. "The ones made from raisins dried in the sun?"

"They are indeed," Sebastiano said. "And do you know our most revered wine, our sherry?"

"A little," I said. "Sherries are fortified wines, aren't they?"

"Yes. Which simply means that grape-based distilled alcohol has been added to wine to bring the alcohol content to at least sixteen percent volume. Then the aging process can begin."

"Why do you suppose the English like sherry so much?"

"Well, for one thing, sherry warms the body. Eighty-percent of our sherry production goes to Great Britain and other northern European countries." He told me he himself preferred the fino and manzanilla sherries, which in Andalusia are usually served chilled. "They're younger and tend to be milder. Tonight if you and your friends have tapas, try *pale fino*. It's dry and light and good as an apéritif."

We continued our ascent into Andalusia's verdant interior, where olive groves stretch as far as the eye can see, silhouetted by the majestic Sierra Nevadas to the east. We saw white-washed villages angled gracefully into the terrain. "That must be one of the *pueblos blancos* (white towns) I've read about," I said.

"Yes," Sebastiano said. "Our fortified hilltop towns date back to Islamic Spain—the Muslims liked to whitewash their buildings to deflect the sun's rays."

I learned that the church towers rising before us once functioned as minarets, and that these houses typically have thick stone-and-mud walls, small windows, and secluded interior courtyards. Today these features are considered shields against heat and cold, but during Islamic times they fulfilled Qur'anic dictates about domestic privacy, especially the seclusion and segregation of women.

I noticed that the houses had shallow-pitched, clay-tiled roofs and small, deeply recessed windows. Sebastiano said that years ago villagers collected their water at a communal well in the town's square, but now all these homes have running water.

Talk of *pueblos blancos* and the surrounding landscape led Sebastiano to tell me about Andalusia's rich *natural* heritage. He estimated that almost twenty percent of Andalusia has been designated as protected land. These reserves offer sanctuary to a vast variety of migratory birds on their long flights between Africa and points north. He showed me Fuente de Piedra (Flamingo Lake) near Antequera, not far off the A-45, the only inland location in Europe where flamingoes can breed. In the spring they congregate by the thousands to reproduce, drawn to the water's high salinity, which facilitates the growth of seaweed and crustaceans, essential to their diet. They also like the lake's shallowness. Sebastiano said that until recently flamingoes in Spain had been under siege. In Roman times, they were hunted for their tongues which were considered a culinary delicacy. Then in the 1930s, the salt company that owned Fuente de Piedra tried to reduce the flamingo population, since they thought the birds' presence undermined the lake's salt production. But once word got out about the lake's ecological value, birdwatchers and naturalistists deluged its shores. To the great relief of ornithologists, in 1988 Fuente de Piedra was officially proclaimed a reserve for birds.

❀

My hotel stood within walking distance of Córdoba's Old Town near the River Guadalquivir, which snakes through the city. From my room, I could see the Roman bridge that spans it. To the south lay wheat fields and olive groves and to the north the soft slopes of the mineral-rich Sierra Morena mountains.

Before joining Tom and Barbara for tapas that evening, I

decided to walk to the old Jewish quarter, the heart of the city. Here I found a labyrinth of narrow, winding, cobblestoned lanes that occasionally afforded glimpses into shaded courtyards festooned with plants, wrought-iron grilles, and ceramic tiles. Houses in the Jewish quarter dated from Spain's Islamic era and, like those I'd seen earlier in the day in the fortified hilltowns, were plain white-washed structures with privacy clearly a key design feature.

In Calle de los Judíos ("Street of the Jews") at the center of the Jewish Quarter, I came across the synagogue built in 1315, one of only three original *sinagogas* remaining in Spain (the other two are in Toledo). This Jewish house of worship became a church in the sixteenth century, after Ferdinand and Isabella expelled the Jews from Spain in 1492.

Jewelry and silversmiths' shops in the neighborhood led to Tiberiadus Square, where I came upon an intriguing statue: a robed and turbaned man, seated, looking pensive, holding a book in his right hand. A quick flip through the pages of my guidebook and I knew that this was the famous Córdoban-born Moses Maimonides (1135-1204), the great Jewish philosopher, scientist, and physician of Andalusia, Morocco, and Egypt. He was born when the Golden Age of Jewish culture in Spain had ended.

My guidebook noted that Jews had lived on the Iberian Peninsula since the third century. The Visigoths persecuted them early on, but after the Arab conquest in the eighth century, Jews assumed key roles in Spanish Muslim society, often serving as administrators, doctors, and businessmen.

Sebastiano helped me understand why interfaith relations were so good during Andalusia's Umayyad dynasty. The Umayyads honored the Qur'anic covenant to protect the *dhimmi*—the protected "Peoples of the Book," fellow monotheistic descendants of the biblical patriarch Abraham who lived under Islamic rule. The Jews were said to have an extraordinary ability to adapt to an Islamic-dominated culture. Under the Umayyads a Jew even served as foreign minister to Abd al-Rahman III, who had declared himself the legitimate Caliph of the Islamic world.

When the radical Almohads seized Córdoba in 1146, they conveniently ignored the Qur'anic dictates about the *dhimmi*, giving its Jewish population three options: convert to Islam, be killed, or go into exile. Maimonides and his family chose exile, living for a time in Morocco, in the Holy Lands, and finally Egypt where he worked as physician to the Grand Vizier Alfadhil and Sultan Saladin of Egypt. There he was deemed the greatest doctor of his time.

Maimonides is also remembered as a brilliant religious philosopher. For example, he was able to reconcile his Jewish faith with a belief in the power of reason, especially Greek philosophy; consequently, he was an important influence on Aquinas and Islamic theologians.

Maimonides died in Egypt in 1204 and was buried in what is today Israel. His epitaph reads: *From Moshe* [of the Torah] *to Moshe* [Maimonides] *there was none like Moshe.*

After touching Maimonides' bronze robe, as a gesture of respect, I continued my walk, stopping at an espresso bar to sip a *café con leche.* I recalled one of Maimonides' Córdoban-born contemporaries, the distinguished Abu al-Walid ibn Ahmad ibn Rushd, known in Europe as Averroës [1128-1198], the medieval Spanish-Arab philosopher, physician, and jurist of the Shar'ia [Islamic] law. While he is revered for his writings on Shar'ia and for reintroducing Aristotle to the West, like Maimonides he is also remembered for his writings on the relationship between faith and reason. He also made the prescient claim that the talents of women might be underused—that women's abilities should not be limited to giving birth and raising children. He believed women capable of leadership, as able as men to be philosopher-rulers, then a major departure from traditional thought.

Like Maimonides, he was born after the intellectual freedoms of the Umayyad times had waned. His theories conflicted with those of the reactionary Almohad Muslims, who loathed books. Tried as a heretic, he was later forced into exile; two years later, he was dead in Marrakesh.

❀

Tom and Barbara are famously prompt. We met in our hotel lobby precisely at the appointed hour of seven. They had just flown in from Barcelona and teemed with tales of that city. However, this evening we decided to concentrate on things Andalusian, most immediately on the region's culinary tradition: tapas—small servings of food eaten before the main course. In France this course is called hors d'oeuvres; in Italy it is called antipasti. Tapas is an Andalusian invention, created to accompany the land's signature drink: sherry. [Sebastiano later told us that Phoenician traders from the East had probably introduced wine into what is now Spain in about 2500 B.C. When Barbara asked how alcohol interfaced with the centuries of Islamic rule, he said that the Qur'an does, indeed, frown on the consumption of alcohol, but that the Moors made wine and consumed it for medicinal purposes.]

Tom had researched a particular tapas bar near our hotel. Once we settled in there, and the waiter came, we all ordered the *pale fino* that Sebastiano had recommended earlier in the day. Then followed a grand array: *almendras fritas* [fried salted almonds], *jamón serrano* [salt-cured ham dried in mountain air], *queso manchego* [sheep's cheese], *tortilla a la española* [Spanish omelette]. The list went on and on.

We asked our waiter about the origins of the tapas. He offered two possible explanations: [1] it originated with a bartender's practice of covering a glass with a saucer or *tapa*

94

[cover] to keep the flies out, which custom then grew to include placing a chunk of cheese or a few nuts on a small tray to accompany a drink; or [2] it is a holdover from Arab rule, since even now in the Middle East tidbits of food are typically served with beverages.

We concluded that both theories made sense, although I favored the fly speculation, since these two-winged insects seemed on a rampage this hot July night.

After our sherry and tapas, we considered going to dinner, but who could eat after all that? Instead we decided to retire early to be ready for Sebastiano's tour at nine the next morning.

❋

Our itinerary for the day began with Córdoba's greatest sight: the aforementioned Great Mosque, the *Mezquita*, which dates back to 785 when Abd al-Rahman I built it to honor his wife.

The site of the Great Mosque was once the Christian Visigothic Cathedral of St. Vincent, and before that, a pagan Roman temple. Near what is now the mosque stood a Visigothic bastion that Abd al-Rahman I took as his residence and government palace, thus, according to Sebastiano, bringing the spiritual and secular hubs of the new emirate into closer proximity. I was intrigued to learn that like Tuscany's Cosimo I de' Medici and his Uffizi, Abd al-Rahman I also feared assassination and, to minimize that risk, built an elevated walkway from his palace to the mosque.

We entered the mosque's prayer hall through an unimposing door with a horseshoe arch that gave no hint of what lay ahead. Once inside, we encountered a vast architectural wonderland of more than eight hundred fifty columns made of jasper, onyx, marble, and granite along with giant horseshoe arches in alternating bands of red and white like holiday candy. Sunlight streamed in through windows in a mesmerizing kaleidoscope of color. We stood breathless. Each visitor, I suppose, leaves with his own take on this elaborate place to pray. Some Arab worshipers have compared its forest of columns to a date-palm grove, a nostalgic touchstone of their distant native soil. But Tom, Barbara, and I cried out to Sebastiano almost in unison: "Why so big?" He spoke of the city's burgeoning size and steady stream of Islamic converts during Córdoba's heyday.

As we stood gazing at this fairyland of pillars and arches, Sebastiano nudged us gently toward the *mihrab*, the spacious and richly gilded prayer niche with its geometric and floral designs in the *qiblah* wall, facing the Ka'ba. "In actuality," Sebastiano confided, "this *qiblah* faces southward as if Abd al-Rahman were still in his beloved Damascus and not in exile." He added, "The *mihrab* is a symbolic entrance to heaven, where worshipers direct their prayers and humble themselves before God." The faithful believe, he told us, that this site symbolizes the Absolute and that it has a way of amplifying the words of the imam [spiritual head of a Muslim community].

I admired the *mihrab's* Byzantine mosaics, the quotations from the Qur'an emblazoned on a blue backdrop, and I especially liked the repetition of floral motifs that Sebastiano said were inspired by Syrian plant life.

Within the confines of the mosque, slightly to our left, a wide space opened up, furnished with beautifully carved monastic choir stalls and an altar—a Catholic cathedral created by the Christians who seized Córdoba in 1236 and drove out the Muslims. They converted the then-defunct mosque into a church. "The Muslims had done the same in 711 when they overran the city, so why not revert to what once was?" Sebastiano said.

This rather startling juxtaposition made sense to me only when I remembered the building's evolution from a pagan Roman temple to a Christian Visigothic church, then to a mosque, and again to a Christian church—this final incarnation completed in 1766.

As a fan of the Baroque period, I appreciated the cathedral's ornate carvings, especially the pulpits by Verdiquier and choir stalls by Pedro Duque Cornejo, made from mahogany imported from the West Indies and Cuba.

We sat for some minutes in the cathedral's pews to absorb the drama surrounding us. Then Sebastiano directed us into the Patio de los Naranjos (Courtyard of the Orange Trees), where the Islamic faithful once conducted their ablutions before prayer. From here I could see the Christian bell-tower, once a minaret used for calling the faithful to worship. Today it's topped with an image of Archangel Raphael, the guardian angel of Córdoba. Sebastiano promised us a sweeping view of the city if we climbed this tower but, given the heat, we declined his offer.

❀

To fully appreciate the grandeur that was once Córdoba, Sebastiano insisted that we ride five miles out of town to see the ruins of Madinah al-Zahra, once a Versailles-like, Arab Muslim palace-town, built into the foothills of the Sierra Morena Mountains by Abd al-Rahman III after he proclaimed himself the Caliph of Córdoba in 929.

As we rode into the Andalusia countryside, Sebastiano noted three traditions of Madinah al-Zahra: (1) Abd al-Rahman III used it to flaunt his wealth and power; (2) the Umayyads used it as a refuge during the violence and political chaos during their nine hundred-year rule; and (3) Abd al-Rahman III built it as a gift to his favorite concubine, Zahra. A legend holds that she complained to her lover about missing the snow-capped mountains of her native Syria. To allay her homesickness, Abd al-Raman III told her: "It will snow for you, Zahra, my love. I shall make it snow for you." He then covered the surrounding hills with white-blossoming cherry and almond trees.

Whichever is true, the town's grandeur was short-lived. Around 1010, during the civil unrest that led to the demise of the Caliphate of Córdoba, an early wave of North African Muslim radicals, vexed by the Umayyads' liberal ways, destroyed Madinah al-Zahra. The town lay buried until 1911, when parts of it were unearthed. Excavation is ongoing, funded by the Spanish government.

As we wandered around the sad remains, I struggled to believe this was once a stupefying palace, with roofs of gold and silver, menageries, and even a pond of quicksilver that flashed rays of light into the atmosphere.

While we drove southwest from Córdoba to Seville, a journey of less than two hours, I asked Sebastiano about Seneca—Lucius Annaeus Seneca [c. 4 B.C.—A.D. 65]—the Córdoban-born philosopher, orator, essayist, playwright, and poet. I'd read that he is considered by some to be the greatest Spaniard ever to have lived. *Why hadn't Sebastiano taken us to see Seneca's commemorative statue in Córdoba?* I wondered. [Sebastiano later explained that Seneca lived centuries before medieval Spain's Golden Age, the focus of our trip; hence he was simply not on the itinerary.]

Hardly had the word *Seneca* spilled from my mouth when Sebastiano beamed. "Such a man!" he said. "He was so multifaceted! A man of letters, a political figure, consul of Rome, Nero's tutor and later counselor, and a Stoic."

"What exactly is a Stoic?" Barbara asked.

"Someone who lives simply, who is moderate and frugal. Someone who makes peace with his present circumstances."

"Are those values you embrace?"

"I try to hold the thought that God determines everything

and that I must accept His will," Sebastiano answered softly.

It was good to hear Sebastiano open up about himself. He was very professional with us. Modest. Self-effacing. He did let drop once that his wife was English, which probably explained his excellent command of the language. He said they make their home in Málaga, and proudly told us they have a daughter with an M.B.A. who works in Dubai.

At some point in Seneca's tenure with Nero, the tutor/counselor apparently crossed his master. The consequence: Nero ordered Seneca to commit suicide, an act the philosopher fulfilled with the grace of a true Stoic, Sebastiano said. Even today some Spanish intellectuals are so caught up in the Seneca mystique that they fancy themselves the philosopher's progeny. "In my case," Sebastiano said, "I wouldn't even feel worthy to touch the great man's hem."

On the subject of stoicism Seneca said: "All cruelty springs from weakness." And another of his epigrams: "Life, if you know how to use it, is long enough." On the subject of applying philosophy to everyday life: "A large library is apt to distract rather than to instruct the learner; it is much better to confine yourself to a few authors than to wander at random over many." And "Our plans miscarry because they have no aim. When a man does not know what harbor he is making for, no wind is the right wind."

Some students of Seneca believe that he might have been an early Christian. He is credited with saying: "Live with men as if God saw you; converse with God as if men heard you." And "God is nigh to you, he is with you, he is in you: I tell you ... a holy spirit resides within us, an observer and guardian of our good and our bad doings, who, as he has been dealt with by us, so he deals with us; no man is good without God."

The earliest name for the site now called Seville (Sevilla in Spanish) is "Tartessus," a town on the River Guadalquivir about eighty-eight miles downriver from Córdoba and built by the Phoenicians about twenty-eight hundred years ago as a trading center.

With each succeeding occupation, Seville held her own. During Arab rule, Córdoba was the capital of al-Andalus, but once social and political strife fractured Andalusia into *taifas*, Seville became the most important of these small political entities. When the radical Almohads took over, they made Seville their capital.

Sebastiano speculated that the city's ability to prevail against the odds resulted from the River Guadalquivir: its port, its adjacent fertile plains, and its access to the Mediterranean, a mere sixty-eight miles away. Under Christian rule Seville benefited from lucrative trade monopolies with the Spanish territories of the New World.

We arrived in Seville late in the afternoon. After settling into our hotel in the Barrio de Santa Cruz (neighborhood of the holy cross), once the city's Jewish Quarter, we planned to rest a bit, then enjoy an Andalusian dinner and take in a flamenco performance. Reservations are a prerequisite in Seville, and as usual Sebastiano had anticipated our wishes. He even joined us for the evening.

Santa Cruz is Seville's most romantic and densely populated neighborhood. Its narrow alleyways are lined with window-grilled white houses and flower-decked courtyards. Occasionally, strolling guitarists entertain. The cavernous Seville Cathedral looms nearby as does the magnificent Alcázar of Seville (royal palace). Santa Cruz vibrates with restaurants and *tablaos* (flamenco clubs) from where that soulful Andalusian art form, flamenco, beckons.

As we walked to our restaurant, Sebastiano told us about the culinary legacies credited to the Moors: *ajo blanco* (almond gazpacho); *cabello de ángel* (pumpkin preserve); the spices cumin, saffron, and anise; and candies made from ground almonds.

Tomatoes arrived after 1492, he noted, from the Spanish colonies in the Americas. Sevillian cuisine is based largely on home recipes. Locals are not great restaurant-goers, Sebastiano said, so it's tourism that keeps Seville's gastronomic culture alive.

On this evening we skipped tapas and went straight for chilled gazpacho garnished with cucumbers, croutons, and red peppers. Our wines were local whites (*blanco*) and reds (*tinto*). Bread came with thick, green olive oil for dipping.

For our main courses, Tom chose *trucha a la Navarra* (baked trout with jamón serrano), Barbara selected *gallina en pepitoria* (braised hen in almond sauce), Sebastiano went for *solomillo de cerdomudéjar* (pork tenderloins with dates and walnuts), and I opted for *huevos a la Flamenca* (baked eggs), a favorite provincial specialty.

For our final course, Sebastiano tried to tempt us with *tocino de cielo* (heavenly delight), which he claimed was one of the best custard-and-caramel desserts on the Iberian Peninsula, but we decided that our dessert would be the flamenco performance to follow.

The *tablao* turned out to be a theater-like space in the back of a bar. Posters picturing flamenco dancers jumped from the walls. Soon there were no empty seats.

As we waited for the performance to begin, Sebastiano characterized flamenco as "a passionate and seductive ritual form of dance that is performed out of happiness or grief," and Barbara asked what sort of grief might evoke such a dance.

"A lament, perhaps. There's a famous one, a *petenera*, that tells of a young girl who brings misfortune to herself and her people." He talked about the intense emotionality of flamenco. "If it's done well," he said, "it can be deeply moving."

Flamenco's origins are obscure, but history suggests that Gypsies brought some version of this art form to Spain from their centuries-long wanderings through India, Iran, Egypt, and North Africa. Today flamenco contains elements of jazz, Latin and rock music, and its choreography has changed, too, but no matter the era, it's always been a major tourist attraction in Seville.

Once the performance began, we were absorbed in the fiery music of the guitarist, the male singer, and the hand-clapper. The *bailaora* (female dancer), who appeared in a flounced, cascading and ruffled polka-dot dress (*batas de colas*), stood still as if absorbing the rhythm of the music; only when the spirit moved her did she begin to dance. She wore dangling earrings, hair combs, high-heeled shoes, and a *mantilla* (lace headscarf). Her wooden castanets kept pace with the guitarist. Throughout the performance, the beautiful *bailaora* dominated, while the male *bailaor* played a supportive role.

As the music grew more spirited, arms and hands gestured spontaneously, while legs and feet attacked the floor with a rapid-fire, staccato rhythm. The more the performance burned with life, the more the audience shouted *¡Olé! ¡Baile! ¡Baile!* (Dance! Dance!)

Much of flamenco is improvised, reflecting the artist's emotions at the moment. Some aficionados actually believe that a spiritual force drives the dancers. "We in Andalusia like to say that we don't *see* flamenco, we *feel* it," Sebastiano said.

On the stroll back to our hotel, Barbara mentioned that she and Tom were fans of Andrés Segovia, the great Spanish classical guitarist (1893-1987). Chuckling with pride, Sebastiano said, "Segovia used to say that he rescued the guitar from the hands of flamenco Gypsies and developed a classical repertoire fit for concert halls."

"He believed his real musical education began after he moved to Granada," Barbara said.

"Yes, he moved there as a teenager and probably fell into the hands of a good teacher. Granada has an excellent university—talented people gravitate there."

I mentioned that I'd read that he described Granada as a "place of dreams, where the Lord put the seed of music in my soul."

"I've heard that quote," Sebstiano said. "I think his source of inspiration might have been *more* than just Granada. It might have been the other-worldly atmosphere of the Alhambra. You'll see for yourself when we visit there in two days. Some people believe that the Alhambra actually casts magic spells—that it enchants."

In Seville, the world's largest Roman Catholic cathedral (Saint Peter's in Rome is a basilica) occupies the site of a twelfth-century Almohad mosque. The only remaining Islamic legacies are La Giralda, once the minaret, now a dark imposing bell-tower, and the Patio de los Naranjos, formerly the site of ablutions before prayer, now an area for reflection.

After entering the cathedral through the Puerta de la Asunción, we immediately felt the welcome coolness that such stone buildings afford.

The length of the nave, the longest in Spain, caught our attention, as did the stained-glass windows, which Tom said reminded him of those he saw in the Sainte Chapelle in Paris. I liked the rose window at the west end of the nave, which depicts in vivid color the four Evangelists.

The religious art of Seville's native son, Bartolomé Esteban Murillo (1617-1682), especially his tender rendering of *El Ángel de la Guarda* (The Guardian Angel) moved us all. We liked Murillo's subtle use of color, the way he highlighted the young Jesus and backlighted the guardian angel.

When we came to the Capilla Mayor with its Gothic *retablo* (altarpiece)—forty-five carved-wood scenes from the life of Christ by the Spanish artist, Pierre Dancart—we stood transfixed. This large altarpiece, protected by a commanding Renaissance grille in gilded bronze, is the cathedral's magnum opus.

Sebastiano then left us to explore the cathedral on our own. I investigated what is reputed to be the tomb of Christopher Columbus, which is held on the shoulders of four figures said to represent the kingdoms of Aragón, León, Castile, and Navarra. Later Sebastiano told me that recent DNA samples confirmed that at least some of Columbus's remains rest within that casket.

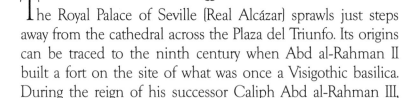

The Royal Palace of Seville (Real Alcázar) sprawls just steps away from the cathedral across the Plaza del Triunfo. Its origins can be traced to the ninth century when Abd al-Rahman II built a fort on the site of what was once a Visigothic basilica. During the reign of his successor Caliph Abd al-Rahman III, the fort took on the added role of governor's residence.

As I have already noted, after the Umayyad dynasty came the Almohads, the Almoravids, and eventually the Christians. Each dynasty left its mark. Today the Royal Palace is striking for its absorbing fusion of Arab/Spanish influences. The upper floors are reserved for Spain's current royal family.

After entering the palace through the Puerta del León (Gate

of the Lion), we were outfitted with audio players that permitted us to move through the premises at our own pace, listening to taped explanations in English. Sebastiano could take a welcome break.

Map in hand, I made my way through the Patio de la Montería (Courtyard of the Hunt), past horseshoe arches to the Patio de las Doncellas (Patio of the Maidens), once the center of official court life. Legend holds that occupying Muslims required that Spain's Christian kingdoms pay an annual tribute of one hundred virgins. (Sebastiano later told us that the legend was more likely a ploy to strengthen the Christian *Reconquista* movement.)

While I liked the many Arab architectural legacies—arches, columns, mosaics, stuccos, plasterworks, and marquetry—I appreciated most the palace's grounds, which, under Muslim rule, produced fresh vegetables. Today this area is a sea of orange trees, jasmine, laurel, and lavender, along with rosebushes and topiary. Interspersed are cisterns, aqueducts, water channels, fountains, and grottoes, which aid irrigation, the much-prized Umayyad-introduced technology.

Water, I knew, has always played an important role in Islam: In the Qur'an, paradise is portrayed as a shaded and enclosed garden where water flows. Muslims' ablutions before prayer are believed to purify the supplicants; hence, all mosques have a space for this cleansing ritual.

❀

Our final Andalusian destination was Granada, which lies at the foot of the Sierra Nevada Mountains, where the rivers Darro and Genil meet. Here we would visit the Alhambra, the last stronghold of Islam's eight-hundred-year physical existence in Europe. It was the palace and fortress of the Nasrids, the final Islamic dynasty (1236-1492) of Europe's Middle Ages.

After the defeat in 1212 of the despised North African Almohads, several Andalusian *taifa*-like factions tried to fill the void created by their departure. But it was Muhammad ibn Yusuf ibn Nasr, also known as Ibn Ahmar, who triumphed. After the Christian conquest of Córdoba in 1236, Ibn Ahmar forged an alliance with the Christian Kingdom of Castile, paying them tribute, in exchange for which they granted him fragile sovereignty over the Nasrid Kingdom of Granada—a sliver of land in the southeastern corner of Spain.

The Nasrids turned the Alhambra into a shimmering fortress, making it the foremost example of Islamic architecture in Europe and one of the finest anywhere in the world. Alhambra became a hotbed of intellectual ferment, with many of its discoveries and suppositions further stoking the Renaissance. But by 1479 Castile and Aragón decided that they wanted Granada with its fairyland Alhambra for themselves. In 1492, the last of the Nasrids, Muhammad XI (also known as Boabdil), surrendered control to the Catholic monarchs, Ferdinand and Isabella, during the Reconquest. (It's from Alhambra, by the way, that these same monarchs sent Christopher Columbus off to discover the New World.)

Historians recount an anecdote about this surrender: As Boabdil left Granada for good, he is reported to have sighed deeply, whereupon his mother denigrated such feminine display of emotion for a homeland that her son did not have the masculinity to defend.

After the Christian takeover, Jews and Muslims were forced to convert to Roman Catholicism or face expulsion or death. Some did convert, most fled. The Castilian language replaced Arabic, Christian churches replaced mosques.

The fall of Granada signified the end of an eight-hundred-year-long Islamic presence in Spain and thus in Europe.

As we drove the nearly three hours from Seville to Granada, I recalled that Washington Irving (of *The Legend of Sleepy Hollow* fame) traveled a similar route in 1829. Only *he* traveled by horseback, probably under the watchful eyes of the road's notorious bandits.

He described the trails then as "little better than mere mule-paths." His valuables had been shipped ahead; he and his fellow traveler had retained only the basic necessities of life, along with a stipend large enough to satisfy the *banditti* who inevitably lurked along the way.

In Sebastiano's comfortable van, we cruised along carefree on superhighways, arriving safely at our hotel around noon. We then headed for the Sierra Nevada spur overlooking Granada on which the Alhambra is situated.

Poets have called the Alhambra "a pearl set in emeralds," and after stepping through the palace's main entrance we understood why. We fell into a sequence of resplendent rooms that seemed to flow from one to the next, as if in a symphonic melody. There were elegant columns, complex stalactite-like ceiling adornments, stylish arabesques, subtle calligraphy, and more arches than I had ever seen—even in Cordóba's Great Mosque.

My favorite space was the *Patio de los Leones* (Court of the Lions), its perimeter lined by arcades supported by one hundred twenty-four slender marble columns. At the center of the court is the Lion Fountain, a stately alabaster basin resting upon twelve marble lions that signify power and fortitude.

"We're not sure where the lions came from," Sebastiano said. "We are certain, however, that the Muslims didn't make them. The Qur'an prohibits the representation of living creatures. Prophet Mohammed feared the return to idolatry. We suspect the lions were crafted by Jewish or Christian artists."

I was fascinated to discover how many Arabic inscriptions found their way into the Alhambra's décor, "which reveals," said Sebastiano, "how thoroughly the Moors' religious views were in lockstep with their art and architecture." He added that the inscriptions in the Alhambra tended to follow three patterns: [1] verses from the Qur'an; [2] traditional expressions of faith; [3] verses lauding the Alhambra's owners/principals. He directed our attention to the inscriptions cut around the fountain's basin, attributed to the statesman Abu Abd Allah ibn-Zamrak [1333-93?]. One of them reads:

May the blessings of God forever be with you! May He make your subjects obedient to your rule, and grant you victory over all your enemies!

The French poet, dramatist, novelist, journalist and literary critic Théophile Gautier [1811-1872], was so taken with the Alhambra's Court of the Lions that he considered replicating it in his Paris garden. After spending nearly five months touring Spain, with Granada a high point, Gautier produced in 1841 a bestseller, *Voyage en Espagne.*

Weaving our way through many of the Alhambra's interiors, we followed a footpath to the Yannat al Arif [known as Generalife Gardens], the Nasrids' country retreat laid out in the thirteenth century, on the north side of the premises.

In these well-manicured gardens, I liked best the spirited fountains, which suggested that the Moors had not forgotten the arid land from which their forebears had come, prizing water above all other life-giving elements.

As we strolled through these cultivated grounds, Sebastiano reminded us that the historical figure Leo Africanus [Al Hassan ibn Muhammad al-Wazzan al-Fassi], Moorish merchant, diplomat, geographer, and author, was born in Granada around 1494, just two years after the last of the Nasrids had surrendered. Given the turmoil of the times, soon after Leo's birth his

Spanish Muslim family fled across the Mediterranean, most probably to the Andalusian quarter of Fez. There he excelled as a student and became a man of many talents. His professional life included service to sultans and popes; it's thought that he might even have inspired Shakespeare's Othello. Sebastiano said that in the eyes of many, Leo's foremost legacy was his book *The History and Description of Africa and of the Notable Things Therein Contained.* In his own eyes, Sebastiano believed that Leo's greatest contribution might well have been his masterful portrayal of the meeting of Islam and Christianity. As a Muslim who lived a good part of his life as a Christian, Leo wrote for Christian readers about Islam.

After Sebastiano's aside on Leo Africanus, he brought us back to the subject at hand—the Alhambra, a place of grace and imagination, reminiscent of Córdoba at its prime.

"As the Nasrid influence dimmed, they seemed to cling all the more to their vision of the Alhambra as a perfect place, a kind of paradise on earth, with Yannat al Arif as 'the garden of lofty paradise.' To them this mountain top citadel offered light to a Europe otherwise still shrouded in darkness. But we all know what happened in 1492, when the last of the Nasrids surrendered control to the Catholic monarchs Ferdinand and Isabella, during the Reconquest."

As we strolled to his van, he concluded nostalgically, "Like all things in life, this seemingly perfect place, too, proved transitory."

❀

After three days in Granada, we made our way back to Málaga and said our goodbyes. Another tour group would soon summon our gentle guide. Tom and Barbara and I would fly back to the U.S. In the hours of my flight, I was happy to have been reminded in Andalusia of what is possible when people set aside their differences and promote what unites them.

I also thought about how timely it was to experience the side of Islam so apparent during medieval Spain's Golden Age, one I came to know during my years in the United Arab Emirates—the innovative, benevolent and tolerant side that has all but vanished from the collective memory of many in recent years.

May the story of the immigrant prince's al-Andalus, for a time a cultural jewel of nearly unrivaled brilliance, rekindle that memory. May it also remind us that peaceful coexistence and cooperation among people are possible.

5

Oxenaforda

"There is nothing in England to be matched with what lurks in the vapours of these meadows, and in the shadows of these spires—that mysterious, inalienable spirit, spirit of Oxford. Oxford! The very sight of the word printed, or sound of it spoken, is fraught for me with most actual magic."

—Max Beerbohm

The telephone's shrill, persistent ring pulled me out of sleep.

"Hello?" I answered groggily as I studied the alarm clock near my bed: 4:12 a.m.

This can't be good news, I thought. To make matters worse, pounding rain outside my bedroom window left no doubt that Seattle was in for another soggy day.

"This is Cara in Rome," my niece choked into the telephone. "Mama had a massive brain hemorrhage in Oxford a few hours ago. She's in the Intensive Care Unit at the John Radcliffe Infirmary. It's the worst bleed doctors have ever seen where a patient has lived. If you want to see Mama again, you best go to Oxford right away."

I recoiled. My head began to whirl. Just a few years before, my husband had lain in an ICU dying of a brain disease. *Now this?* I didn't want to believe it.

I knew that Cara's mother, my beloved younger sister, Anne, had gone from her home in Belgium to Oxford, England, the week before to help with her newly born granddaughter. I knew that for days and weeks prior to her departure she had had relentless headaches for which her doctor in Brussels had merely prescribed painkillers. I tried to come to terms with the dreadful news.

"I'm so sorry," I gulped to Cara when I found my voice again. I tried to extract every last morsel of information about Anne's condition, forgetting that she, a young, housebound mother in Rome, could only have learned of the Oxford crisis long-distance herself. She could only repeat that her father had said the situation was grave and that she, too, would fly to England as soon as she could make childcare arrangements for her toddler.

"Thanks for letting me know," I moaned as we ended our conversation.

Since it was early November, the off-season, airlines were only too happy to accommodate my last-minute need for a Seattle-London ticket, and thus delivered me, in the late afternoon of the next day, to London's Heathrow Airport. I then taxied fifty-four miles northwest to Oxford's Warnborough Road, where Anne's son, my nephew Eric, the proud father of the new baby girl, lived with his wife, and two sons under the age of seven.

After heartfelt hellos to this stricken family and a quick deposit of my luggage into the guestroom upstairs, Anne's husband, Paxton, walked me along Oxford's already darkened streets to the John Radcliffe Infirmary ["the JR"] on Woodstock Road. Here family members could be with their loved ones twenty-two hours a day.

Anne lay intubated. Tubes coiled out of her brain, spilling dark blood into a plastic receptacle behind her head.

"She is not out of danger yet," Anne's doctor told us soon after we arrived. To underscore the seriousness of her condition, he added: "Her brain is bleeding in three places."

He went on to explain that the blood's darkness suggested *old* blood, as if Anne's brain had been bleeding internally for some time. It began to pool, he speculated, creating pressure, thus the debilitating headaches she had experienced prior to her trip to Oxford.

❁

I spent my first hours and days in Oxford focused single-mindedly on Anne's condition. Each morning around eight as I marched from Warnborough Road to the JR, I took only cursory notice of the city's honey-colored skyline of towers, pinnacles, and spires looming around me. I hardly cared that this was the seat of England's illustrious University of Oxford (informally Oxford University), a learning center since about 1167, and now a federation of thirty-six colleges specializing in the humanities, which has graduated over two dozen British prime ministers, assorted kings, and Nobel Prize winners. President Clinton attended as a Rhodes Scholar. That the University of Oxford had also educated such luminaries as John Donne (1572-1631), Joseph Addison (1672-1719), Percy Bysshe Shelley (1792-1822), and Matthew Arnold (1822-1888) seemed a mere curiosity. I felt indifferent when a neighbor showed me the house where Clinton lived years before. To my distraught mind then, such references seemed completely irrelevant.

From experience I knew that during moments of high drama we can feel strangely detached from our immediate surroundings, as if the mind and emotions have temporarily parted ways, retreating from reality while adjusting to the crisis.

During this period, when only Anne seemed to matter, I arrived at the ICU one morning to find that her endotracheal tube had been removed. She could breathe on her own. She was conscious. She knew her name. She knew my name. Her four languages appeared to be intact (in Brussels Anne worked as a translator for the European Commission).

"Anne stands a good chance of making a full recovery," her doctor announced, clearly surprised by the sudden turn of events.

Given the improved prognosis, our state of paralysis eased. Paxton returned part-time to his office in Brussels; Eric to his workplace in London, coming to visit his mother in the ICU on his way home each night. Knowing that Anne would remain in the JR for some time more, I stayed on in Oxford to keep her company.

With the doctor's positive outlook, a veil seemed to have lifted. It was as though the doctor had suddenly given me permission to take notice of Oxford proper, a comfortable walk from the JR. Before, I had stumbled almost unconsciously from Eric's home to the hospital. Now, during the morning hours, when family members had to vacate the ICU so the staff could bathe the patients and conduct medical procedures (usually from 9 to 11, sometimes until noon), I sipped coffee at Starbucks on Cornmarket Street, and explored this ancient town.

I visited Blackwell's, Oxford's esteemed bookstore on Broad Street, which claims to hold 250,000 volumes. I discovered High Street, often called "the High," on which five colleges front, along with the mighty Oxford University Press Bookshop. The High's antique silver stores always caught my attention. What a contrast: Anne's dire straits in the hospital just blocks away, and these glistening objects! The sight of Oxford students in their flapping academic gowns, often on antiquated bicycles, always reminded me of my own college days—happy, carefree days with no thoughts of ICUs, death and dying.

When the sun shone, I stole moments along the River

114

Thames, which for about ten miles in and around Oxford is known as the Isis. Along its shores I breathed in the crisp November air, imagining how, in summer, punts might drift languidly along this waterway. As I daydreamed in this peaceful setting, I remembered too how, paradoxically, in times of strife, I have found solace by immersing myself in beauty—as if it carried with it certain medicinal properties that could lift a battered spirit. Plotinus said, "He who beholds beauty becomes beautiful." *Maybe that's why I gravitated to Florence after John's death—the beauty of that place, its sensuality, its spirituality.* I had left Florence renewed.

Slowly, terms such as "The Carfax Tower," "Radcliffe Camera," "the Bridge of Sighs," "Sheldonian Theatre," and "Ashmolean Museum" took hold in my mind. Although *The Chronicles of Narnia* had long been familiar to me, I had forgotten that its author, C.S. Lewis [1893-1963], had taught at Oxford's Magdalen College. I had forgotten, too, that J.R.R. Tolkien [1992-1973] [*Lord of the Rings*] and Lewis Carroll [1832-98] [*Alice in Wonderland*] had both been Oxford dons. Cecil Rhodes, [1853-1902] the founder of the Rhodes Scholarship, is said to have viewed the University of Oxford as a finishing school for supermen. That this town had been home to giants slowly began to sink in. Oxford was no longer just about the ICU; it was now an enticing universe to explore.

I went to Blackwell's and bought an Oxford guidebook and some other related travel pieces, one of which said that we journey in part to hone the edges of our lives, to dampen our complacencies, maybe even to taste a little hardship. In Oxford I suffered no hardship—that had been reserved to Anne, unfortunately—but I rather liked the simplicity that suddenly confronted me. I had left my own domestic cares behind. My neighbors looked after my house; I paid my bills electronically. In a heartbeat, I had been tossed across the world where even a short walk began to thrill me. At home I live a relatively predictable life, but here I was prey to a certain randomness. Other than spending time in the ICU and with Eric's young family, *chance* had unexpectedly become a major player in my life and I liked it.

Didn't John Lennon say that life is what happens to us while we're busy making other plans?

❀

One morning at Starbucks, I sat reading *The International Herald Tribune*, when I found myself suddenly awash in the sweet melodies of the American South. From a table nearby, I heard lively *y'alls* and two or three *ahs* in lieu of the first person *I.* I heard *reckon* in place of *think.* ["Ah reckon we ought to be gettin' back to class."] I heard *fixin'* to imply a future action, and when I couldn't tell if I'd heard *guard* instead of *god,* or *sore* instead of *saw,* I looked up.

Before me sat three strapping young men—university students? I wondered—talking animatedly with one another. I couldn't resist asking the one nearest me, "Where are you from?"

"Atlanta," he intoned in a soft Georgia drawl. "Dallas," offered another. The third, "Richmond, Virginia."

"And how about you?" the Virginia youth volleyed back to me.

"Seattle," I answered, feeling immediate kinship with my fellow countrymen and their wonderful range of accents. I went on to explain that while I now lived in the Pacific Northwest, I had gone to college in the South and had developed a deep affection for it. "I still delight in Southern American English, so I couldn't resist saying hello when I heard you speak."

They seemed as happy as I to have connected with another American. We exchanged first names and outlined briefly what brought each of us to Oxford.

They were, indeed, University of Oxford students–graduate

students—and two were members of its rowing team, the Oxford University Boat Club. I told them about Anne and the ICU.

Wythe, the Dallas fellow, identified himself as a medical student. When he heard that Anne's endotracheal tube had been removed, he offered, "That's a good sign. In all likelihood, she'll make it now."

"Thanks, Wythe," I sighed, "I need all the hope I can get."

I asked about rowing. Braden, the Virginian, said, "Oxford and Cambridge have been battling against each other over four and a quarter miles on the River Thames since 1829. Richard [the Atlanta youth] and I row in that battle. Wythe *would* row with us, but his medical rotations preclude that kind of extracurricular activity for now."

After a few more friendly exchanges, my new acquaintances dashed to their classes, leaving me to my newspaper.

Starbucks was my sanctuary. It's where I could just be me. There were no expectations. In the ICU all attention focused on Anne. At the house on Warnborough Road the family happily consumed me; the minute I walked in the door the boys wanted to play and the baby needed to be held. But today I decided to explore the erstwhile haunts of one of Oxford's most acclaimed sons, the poet Matthew Arnold, alumnus of the distinguished Balliol College, academic home to such other bright lights as Aldous Huxley, Graham Greene, and prime ministers Edward Heath and Harold Macmillan.

As an English literature major, I had studied Matthew Arnold, never imagining that someday I would linger in his *city of dreaming spires*, the phrase he crafted in the poem "Thyrsis," his elegy for Arthur Hugh Clough, with whom he'd shared many Oxford days.

I especially liked Arnold's reference to Oxford as a "sweet city," an impression I was rapidly embracing. Its architectural beauty and manageable size—a population of about 165,000—

gave the town a comfortable environment. And increasingly, as I came to know who had studied here, I began to pay more attention to the university's centuries-old reputation for academic excellence.

Among Matthew Arnold's favorite Oxford settings was Port Meadow, a vast low-lying common area just northwest of the town center, where he liked to walk with his children. From Eric I learned that in summer this meadow is grazing land for horses and cattle, but it's also used for recreational activities such as walking, kite-flying, biking, and punting. In late spring it becomes a carpet of buttercups, and in winter it turns into floodlands, coveted by fearless canoeists. When the floodlands freeze over, they become a skater's paradise.

One November afternoon I decided to walk out to Port Meadow, which had inspired not only Matthew Arnold, but also Gerard Manley Hopkins (1844-1889), Kenneth Grahame (1859-1932), and T. E. Lawrence (1888-1935). When my little nephews heard where I was going, they begged to come along. They knew that even in winter, horses roam the area freely.

When we arrived, we saw canoeists glorying in the torrent the local river had become; the horses, however, moved guardedly as if thrown off by winter's surge.

As we walked Port Meadow's periphery, I could easily imagine why writers were drawn to this vastness with its stillness and calm—and its long history. I had read that these fields, which have never been ploughed, have yielded round barrows from the Bronze Age and artifacts from Iron Age settlements. Eric told me that a visiting American scholar once asked an Oxford historian to show him the town's most celebrated ancient monument. The historian pointed to Port Meadow.

A brisk wind began to stir. Clouds gathered. Jeff and Lee grew cold. We raced for Warnborough Road and the family that awaited us.

✳

It was fun to be in Europe, yet in an English-speaking country. No struggles with French or Italian here—only English, whose roots reached to the invading Germanic tribes of fifteen hundred years ago when they crossed the English Channel in search of new lands. To think that these rag-tag tribesmen laid the foundation of what is today the world's lingua franca! One of Anne's doctors amused me when she referred to the Europeans [those on the Continent] as "they" and the English along with the North Americans as "we."

Eric's house on Warnborough Road lay in the heart of old Oxford, first mentioned as "Oxnaforda" in the *Anglo-Saxon Chronicle* of 912. It took its name from a ford in the river where oxen crossed.

Without its illustrious university, what would Oxford be today? An industrial center, perhaps, manufacturing the MG, the Mini, the less known Morris Minor. Say *Oxford* to anyone outside Great Britain, and it conjures up a vision of distinguished academics at a most prestigious university. Indeed, its graduates have brought their intellect and influence to bear world-wide.

Within the county seat of Oxford, however, is a long-standing rivalry between "town" and "gown," which has occasionally become violent.

The University of Oxford's concentration of young students, many from privileged backgrounds and with a fondness for alcohol, has long been a source of vexation for ordinary townspeople who have to concentrate on economic survival. As far back as 1209, there is a record of city-dwellers attacking Oxford students, causing them to seek refuge in Cambridge, where a new university soon emerged. Skirmishes ensued again in 1236, 1238, and 1244. In 1298, after several deaths, townspeople complained to the king that some who passed

119

themselves off as students were in fact fugitives from the law. In 1355, "snappish words" and "saucy language" caused still another uproar. And so it went through the centuries. Today the authorities have a firm grip on Oxford, but that does not preclude occasional town-and-gown scuffles.

From Eric's house, I could walk everywhere. I passed Britain's first official museum, the Ashmolean (opened in 1683), on my way home each day. In fact, on this day, after I hurried through the Covered Market—a series of vegetable stalls and small shops tenanted by florists, fishmongers, and bakers—buying fresh dill and scallions for our family lunch, I stopped at the Ashmolean for a quick introductory look.

Originally, the Ashmolean collection consisted of rarities brought back to England by two John Tradescants, sixteenth-century father-and-son traders and explorers. These early artifacts now rest in the University Museum on Park Street. I had come to see the modern Ashmolean, completed in 1845, on Beaumont Street. It had the feel of a Greek temple that urgently needed cleaning. I had read that the Ashmolean receives generous donations. *Why do the British wait so long to freshen their buildings?* I wondered, as I thought of other structures in the UK that I wanted to take a scrub brush to.

On this my first visit, I wanted to view the gold-enameled ornament known as the Alfred Jewel. Over a thousand years old, it was crafted in the reign of Alfred the Great, king of the West Saxons (871-99), and is inscribed *AELRED MEC HEHT* which means "Alfred ordered me made." The two-and-a-half inch relic shows the likeness of a man, possibly Christ, surrounded by religious symbols. Historians think it might have been part of a pointer stick, or a crown, or a brooch.

The Alfred Jewel was found in 1693 in Somerset on land owned by Sir Thomas Wroth near where King Alfred took refuge from the Vikings in 878. It eventually passed into the hands of Sir Thomas's maternal uncle, Colonel Nathaniel Palmer. After the Colonel's death, around 1718, it was presented to the University of Oxford.

I took a brief detour to another wing of the Ashmolean to view Turner's *Venice: The Grand Canal,* painted in 1840. While a student in Florence, I had made occasional trips to Venice where I grew to appreciate Turner's ability to capture its sea and sky in every weather. In the Ashmolean rendering, he melded with electrifying drama these two forces of nature, with brilliant touches of gold as if heaven and earth had merged. I especially liked his take on the buildings of Venice in the background, as if suspended and otherworldly, solidly divine.

As I walked home to Warnborough Road and admired again the staggering array of domes, pinnacles, and towers overhead, I felt so grateful that no Nazi bombs had fallen here. Some historians think that Hitler planned to make Oxford the headquarters for his occupation of Britain—a situation not unlike that of Heidelberg, Germany where Anne and I grew up, which was untouched by Allied bombs and became the headquarters for the U.S. Army in Europe after Germany's unconditional surrender in May 1945. The Allies had also planned ahead.

During my meanderings, I was often struck by the neglected appearance of Oxford's many graveyards: listing tombstones, sunken graves, and the absence of any familial commemoration. Even recent interments seemed soon to fuse with those from generations past. What a contrast to Germany, where family members maintain gravesites over each succeeding generation!

As the gray November mist dampened my cheeks, I wondered how Oxford would look in spring. Would this picturesque town indeed become the symphony of daffodils "Tossing their heads in sprightly dance" that William Wordsworth [1770-1850] described? ["Yes, we find ourselves ablaze in daffodils," Eric told me when I asked him later.)

At home I found Eric's wife, Cate, holding the baby in her left arm while setting the kitchen table with her free arm. I unpacked my parcel of fresh dill and scallions, and together we prepared to make farfalle with smoked salmon and dill for our lunch. We plunged into slicing and sautéing onions in butter, adding wine, cream, salt, pepper, and nutmeg; cutting the smoked salmon into one-inch squares and stirring them into the sauce along with the freshly bought dill; we then boiled the pasta and added it to the sauce. Presto! Lunch was ready.

After lunch I returned to the ICU where Anne slept. Her nurse said that over the last two days Anne had been so stimulated by our visits and doctors' proddings that she was now sleep-deprived and needed rest. With that, I decided to check out the Shelley Memorial on the corner of High Street and Magpie Lane, near University College, from which Percy Bysshe Shelley (1792-1822) was "sent down" (expelled) in 1811, after publishing an anti-religious pamphlet, *The Necessity of Atheism*.

From the JR, I turned right onto Woodstock Road, then left onto Broad Street, and then made another right onto Catte Street and Radcliffe Square, which many consider to be the heart of Oxford. Here I wanted to see the Radcliffe Camera, a Baroque rotunda designed as a memorial to John Radcliffe (1650-1714), the royal physician of William III and Queen Mary. Acclaimed as a diagnostician and medical innovator, Radcliffe early on advocated fresh air over blood-letting. His personal fortune helped finance the infirmary where Anne convalesced, as well as libraries, hospitals, traveling fellowships for medical students, and a college quadrangle.

The Radcliffe Camera is now the main reading room of the nearby Bodleian Library, one of Britain's six copyright deposit libraries, authorized to receive a copy of every book published in Britain. (In the United States, the Library of Congress in

Washington, D.C., serves this function.]

I next came across Saint Mary the Virgin Church, the university's own parish church. When I climbed its tower to get an aerial view of the town, now glazed by fresh rain, I saw that the colleges were arranged around cloistered quadrangles. Gardens, sports fields, and bucolic meadows accented the panorama.

After crossing the High, I finally landed at the foot of Shelley's celebrated memorial. Shelley's Oxford career had been short-lived. He arrived on campus in 1810 as the prospective heir of a baronetcy, but was soon dismissed as a "ringleader of every species of mischief in our grave walls." Always eccentric and nonconformist, he decided early to devote his life to resisting injustice and oppression. He dabbled in the supernatural, conducting experiments that caused others to label his rooms there a sorcerer's den. Experimenting with gunpowder, he once blew the lid off his desk during a lesson. He voiced radical political views and dressed outlandishly. But what cost him his place at Oxford were his inflammatory writings, especially the aforementioned *Necessity of Atheism,* which denies God's existence since it cannot be confirmed by empirical findings. Dubbed "Mad Shelley," he was disinherited by his father, divorced by his first wife, and generally considered a pariah in England. In 1818, at age 26, Shelley left his native land to begin a new life in Italy.

For a time he seemed to have found contentment in and around Pisa, with his "Pisan Circle" that included friends such as George Gordon, Lord Byron [1788-1824]. However, this interval ended quickly. On July 8, 1822, while living at Lerici, Shelley drowned in a boating accident. A few days later, his body washed ashore at Viareggio just north of Pisa and was cremated on the beach in Byron's presence.

About a year before his own death, Shelley completed a poem called "Adonais," an elegy on the passing of his friend

John Keats, whom he ranked "among the writers of the highest genius who have adorned our age."

Shelley was buried in Rome's Protestant cemetery, *Cimitero Acattolico*, a place the poet once described as so beautiful "it might make one in love with death, to be buried in so sweet a place." After Shelley died, Byron portrayed his young friend as "the best and least selfish man I ever knew. I never knew one who was not a beast in comparison."

While living in Italy in the mid-1990s, I visited Shelley's final resting place near Rome's Pyramid of Caius Cestius, where cats slink among the cypresses. In a secluded corner of this preserve, I found Keats's resting place as well. Filled with an apparent bitterness at what his brief life had garnered, Keats's tombstone reads: *This Grave contains all that was Mortal of a YOUNG ENGLISH POET, Who on his Death Bed, in the Bitterness of his Heart at the Malicious Power of his Enemies, Desired these Words to be engraven on his Tomb Stone. Here lies One Whose Name was writ in Water. Feb. 24th 1821.*

The Shelley Memorial in Oxford was intended for his grave in Rome, but the Italian authorities deemed it too vulgar for such a consecrated setting. The lifesize white marble sculpture depicts Shelley reclining nude, dead after his drowning. Although expelled from Oxford's University College, Shelley is one of its most famous alumni, honored with this sculpture in a stately domed late-Victorian chamber.

After thinking about the brilliant but troubled life of the genius who was Shelley, I felt emotionally drained. Still, my visit to the ICU on my way home revived me: I found Anne awake and animated.

"How was your day?" she asked.

"It was good," I said, suddenly energized by what I saw before me—Anne increasingly on the mend.

One evening Eric brought home *Shadowlands* on DVD, which we viewed after the children had gone to bed. It immediately struck us that this 1950s mid-life love-story of C.S. Lewis, the honored Oxford don, and his marriage to the American poet Joy Gresham occurred just a few miles from where we were sitting that very moment.

On the following weekend, Eric, the boys and I drove the four miles to The Kilns—a rambling, brick house with many rooms and several fireplaces—where C.S. Lewis lived from October 11, 1931, until his death on November 22, 1963, also the day that President John F. Kennedy died. In Lewis's day a nine-acre garden, pond, and tennis court adjoined the house, but by the time we saw it, most of the grounds had been sold to developers. In 1984 the house itself was acquired by the C.S. Lewis Foundation to become the site of a Christian study center. Still, Eric and I felt glad to visit the place where Lewis wrote such classics as *The Chronicles of Narnia, Surprised by Joy, A Grief Observed, The Screwtape Letters, The Great Divorce,* and *Mere Christianity.*

One of our Warnborough Road neighbors is involved with the C.S. Lewis Foundation and told us that many children still write to thank Lewis for his *Chronicles of Narnia.* One American boy, upon hearing that Lewis had passed away, nonetheless began his letter: "Dear Mr. Lewis, I'm sorry you died."

Nearly all children's letters ask, "What inspired you to write *The Chronicles of Narnia?*"

The answer is in his essay, "It All Began with a Picture"; indeed, the answer is in its title. From the time Lewis was sixteen, he had an image of a faun in a snowy wood, carrying an umbrella and packages. A quarter of a century later, he decided to create a story from the picture, helped by his recent dreaming of lions. Thus ensued *The Chronicles of Narnia.*

During my morning visits to Starbucks, I often ran into my new acquaintances from the American South. Mainly I saw Braden, the blond, six-foot-three student from Virginia, who said he needed a caffeine buzz in order to perform optimally. He thought caffeine to be the best mood-altering drug in the world, far better than nicotine and alcohol. One day he invited me to accompany him on his walk to Christ Church College, the largest of the thirty-six in the University of Oxford federation.

I had not yet seen this campus, which my guidebook said is considered the grandest of all, and which has produced sixteen British prime ministers in the last two hundred years. We moved along Cornmarket Street, passing Carfax Tower, the remains of the fourteenth-century Church of Saint Martin and today a popular Oxford meeting place, just when its clock struck the quarter hour. We crossed High Street and found ourselves arriving moments later at the Meadow Building, entrance to Christ Church. Standing inside the Great Quad, with its golden-toned buildings, Braden told me that Cardinal Wolsey established Christ Church (originally called Cardinal's College) in 1525 to advance humanistic studies. Its chapel is actually a *cathedral*, Christ Church Cathedral, the smallest in England, yet a big chapel for a college. Suddenly, Braden looked at his watch and cried: "My God! I'm late for my appointment with my tutor. See you at Starbucks." We waved a hasty goodbye and then I stepped into the cathedral to rest among its pews and absorb its mesmerizing stillness.

After my rest, I walked to the adjacent water-meadows that reach to one of the Thames's tributaries. The upper meadows, those closest to the college, which owns them, are sports fields; the lower meadows are used for grazing cattle.

As I wandered, I thought about one of Braden's favorite Christ Church alumni: Charles Lutwidge Dodgson (Lewis Carroll), who for forty-seven years was a mathematician and logician at the college, first as undergraduate, then as faculty.

Braden liked best Carroll's "Jabberwocky," the nonsense poem that eventually appeared in *Through the Looking Glass*. "I like Lewis's facility at word play and fantasy," he said. "'Jabberwocky' sprang out of a simple evening he spent with cousins. To while time away after dinner, they played games of verse-making, and 'Jabberwocky' was Lewis's contribution."

I asked him to recite some lines, and he then regaled me with two stanzas that Alice in *Through the Looking-Glass* had to hold up to a mirror in order to read:

> *Twas brillig, and the slithy toves*
> *Did gyre and gimble in the wabe;*
> *All mimsy were the borogoves,*
> *And the mome raths outgrabe.*
>
> *Beware the Jabberwock, my son!*
> *The jaws that bite, the claws that catch!*
> *Beware the Jubjub bird and shun*
> *The frumious Bandersnatch!*

I didn't need caffeine to get a buzz after hearing Carroll's fanciful whimsy.

❁

One morning in early December I arrived at the ICU to hear Anne's doctor announce: "Your sister is now stable enough to be transferred to a regular patient ward here. She'll be moved by noon."

Ecstatic, I called Cate and asked her to alert the family to the good news.

As always, I had to vacate the ICU from 9 to 11 a.m., but given Anne's impending transfer, I decided to spend the morning nearby.

Just minutes from the JR is Oxford's Bridge of Sighs, the steeply arched Hertford Bridge on New College Lane that joins the Old and New Quadrangles of Hertford College. It took its nickname from the bridge in Venice, which it resembles.

One day I met an elderly Welsh woman who said the Bridge of Sighs in Venice had so affected her that she fell victim to the "Stendhal Syndrome"—rapid pulse, dizziness, and confusion when overcome by beauty—a condition first identified by the nineteenth-century French author who described such symptoms during his visit to Florence in 1817. The Welsh woman said, "I became so overwhelmed by the sheer quantity and beauty of the art at the Uffizi Gallery, that I had to be given smelling salts. An aide told me it was probably the Stendhal Syndrome."

I told her that having lived in Florence, I could well understand this tourist phenomenon.

Near the Oxford Bridge of Sighs, I'd noticed a small bookshop showcasing in its window a book titled *Great Artists from Giotto to Turner,* by Tim Marlow with Phil Grabsky and Philip Rance. I ventured into the shop, examined the book, bought it, then made my way back around the corner to Starbucks to digest it.

Marlow's introduction cites the movement of art away from the province of aristocrats who believed in universal truths that transcended differences among locales and cultures. In the 1970s and 1980s, what he calls "The New Art History" began to take into account the particulars of the environment in which a work of art is created: the political, social and economic milieu.

This was music to my ears. I recalled that in the 1960s as a graduate student in English Literature, I received a B, not the hoped-for A, on a term paper because I had been "too biographical" in my analysis of a particular literary work. I had probed too deeply into the author's environment. How can you separate an artist from his life—from the social, economic, and creative environments in which he lived?

Marlow devotes an entire chapter to Turner, whose painting *Venice: the Grand Canal* I'd sought out at the Ashmolean weeks before. I looked forward to taking this book with me on future visits there.

When I returned to the ICU just after 11 a.m., Anne had already been moved. A nurse told me how to negotiate the hospital's many twists and turns until I found Anne lying in her bed glowing, as if rather pleased with her progress.

❀

"Did you know that penicillin, the world's first antibiotic, was discovered in Oxford?" asked Edmonda, Eric's next-door neighbor and a medical researcher at an Oxford hospital. We were walking her daughter and my nephews along Warnborough Road to the neighborhood play group.

She reminded me that in 1929 Alexander Fleming, a doctor and researcher at St. Mary's Hospital in London, published a paper on a chemical called penicillin and its germ-killing power. Then in 1938, three University of Oxford biomedical investigators—Howard Florey, Ernst Chain and Norman Heatley—decided to build on Fleming's earlier findings by researching ways to grow, extract, and purify enough penicillin to enable its use as a drug.

By the time World War II erupted, their research had borne fruit. And by 1941, when the Nazi Blitzkrieg began assaulting England, they moved penicillin research and production to the United States for safety.

"Had the three Oxford investigators not taken the initiative in 1938 to expand Fleming's earlier discoveries," Edmonda added, "the world's first miracle drug would not have been developed—at least not then." She paused for a moment. "Penicillin came just at the right time—when an infection could as easily have taken the life of a wounded soldier as his wound."

When we reached the play group, housed in an old converted church, we deposited the children, watched them settle into class, and then wandered back to Warnborough Road. En route, Edmonda continued her high-energy tutorial.

"Did you know that Mensa was founded here in Oxford in 1946?"

"No."

"Do you know what it is?"

"A high-IQ society, isn't it?" I said. "We have it in the States, too, but I didn't know that its origins lay here. Who is an English Mensa member that I might know of?"

"Stephen Hawking?"

"You mean the physicist?

"Yes. He was born right here in Oxford in 1942, and attended University College, but eventually switched to the University of Cambridge where he now holds the post once held by Sir Isaac Newton."

After hearing about still another Oxford luminary, I decided to draw Edmonda out on the *supermen*, to borrow Cecil Rhodes's term, who have gravitated to this small English town to prepare for greatness.

"What is it about Oxford, do you think, that attracts prodigies, midwifes them, and births titans?" I asked.

She thought for a moment and said: "This university carries with it an eight hundred year-old mystique that many parents covet for their children. Some would kill to have their sons and daughters admitted to a university that has graduated so many prime ministers and is home to kings and Nobel Prize winners.

130

Others would kill just to have their kids rub shoulders with the world's best and brightest, or simply to make connections that could serve their offspring throughout their lives. You know, only the most gifted get into Oxford. It's based on an admissions process that begins at age twelve—at least in the UK—where students are sorted according to ability. In the end, what goes on here is nothing more than the polishing of an already very bright diamond."

Before reaching home, I asked Edmonda still another question: "On the subject of the genius that seems to emanate from these parts, what do you make of the continued doubts surrounding the authorship of Shakespeare's writings?" I mentioned that I had read in one of the books from Blackwell's that among the most likely "true Shakespeares" was one Edward de Vere, the seventeenth Earl of Oxford (1550-1604).

"Yes," Edmonda said. "The Earl of Oxford was highly educated, widely traveled, a courtier, and an accomplished poet, playwright, and literary patron. During his lifetime in England, it was an unwritten code of the court that Tudor aristocrats were not allowed to publish their creative writings." She added, "In those days it would have been unseemly for a titled man to write for a public theater. To save face, he needed a pseudonym, which might well have been Shakespeare."

"But there must be flaws in that theory?" I said.

"The most prominent is that the Earl of Oxford died in 1604, whereas Shakespeare lived until 1616—supposedly writing plays until about 1613. Those who support the Earl of Oxford theory say that the plays performed for the first time after Oxford's death in 1604 were all written earlier and 'released' during the years following his death." Edmonda concluded in her brisk no-nonsense way, "Too many evidentiary gaps exist to ever bring definitive closure to the Shakespeare authorship question."

As we parted, she to go to work and I to the JR, I contemplated this, still another remarkable Oxford discovery (the Earl of Oxford earned a master's degree from the University of Oxford in 1566).

❦

On an overcast Saturday, Eric, his family, and I drove to nearby Blenheim Palace, which some call England's Versailles. Built between 1705 and 1722, this grand country manor belonged to General John Churchill, First Duke of Marlborough, and commemorated his victory against the French in 1704 at Blenheim, a Bavarian town on the Danube. This Baroque masterpiece is also distinguished as the birthplace and ancestral home of Winston Churchill (1874-1965), British statesman, historian, biographer, and Nobel Prize for Literature laureate.

Cate bundled up baby Lauren and on a breezy December day all six of us roamed a few of the two thousand acres, which once served as royal hunting grounds for Saxon kings. We examined the Grand Bridge, we marveled at the Column of Victory, and we gazed at the Temple of Diana where Winston Churchill is said to have proposed marriage to his future bride, Clementine Hozier.

Lancelot "Capability" Brown (1716-1783), master landscape architect, and instigator of Europe's back to nature movement, designed the palace grounds. Until he came along, the English had no landscape style of their own; they simply copied the formal gardens of the French.

Capability Brown tried to imitate nature so closely that his end result could be mistaken for it. Thus, he had no qualms about changing topography altogether. At Blenheim Park, for example, he actually dammed a stream in order to create two magnificent lakes.

Thomas Jefferson is said to have visited Blenheim Park to study Capability Brown's design before landscaping Monticello.

His notes say: "Their sunless climate has permitted them to adopt what is a beauty of the first order in landscape. Their canvas is of open ground, variegated with clumps of trees distributed with taste ...."

To make ends meet, the Dukes of Marlborough have lately opened Blenheim Palace and its grounds to commercial enterprises, such as a maze, adventure playground, mini-train, gift shops, butterfly house, and fish facility. Without question, for my little nephews, the day's highlight was Blenheim's Adventure Playground.

Before returning home, I asked Eric to stop at Winston Churchill's burial site at St. Martin's Church in Bladon, just outside the Blenheim estate. I wanted to see the final resting place of yet another local superstar. We found Winston Churchill interred with his wife, Clementine, near his parents, Lord Randolph Churchill and American-born Lady Jennie Churchill. Winston Churchill's tombstone reads: "I am ready to meet my Maker. Whether my Maker is prepared for the great ordeal of meeting me is another matter."

As time went by at the JR, I heard talk among Anne's doctors of transferring her to a hospital in Brussels, her home.

My Oxford days waned. I had been called to this gentle English town to witness a possible death; instead, I was privileged to witness a resurrection. And in the process, I made an unforgettable discovery: Oxford itself.

While I'd spent nearly five weeks in this wonderful town, I still had much to discover: I hadn't even set foot into industrial Oxford. And what about the Oxford of PBS's Inspector Morse? Because of the dreary fall weather, I'd bypassed Oxford's gardens, especially the classic seventeenth-century walled Botanic Garden, which sits majestically in the center of Oxford.

And I hadn't begun to explore Oxford's fascinating multi-cultural enclaves.

But I've made up for lost time. On more than one occasion, I've stopped off in Oxford en route to Brussels to visit Anne, who has made an astonishing recovery.

6
Jerusalem

Yerusháláyim (in biblical Hebrew)

Al-Quds (in Arabic)

"The world has ten measures of beauty, and nine of these belong to Jerusalem."

—Jerusalem adage

When friends ask why I keep returning to Jerusalem (I've been there four times), my answer always begins by mentioning its physical beauty, especially in the spring. In that season, the rock-strewn Judean hills surrounding the city turn a soft rain-fresh green, providing pastureland for grazing sheep. Accenting this panorama are masses of wildflowers, with the scarlet anemone among the most prolific, creating carpets of red. Some say the scarlet anemone denotes the "lilies of the field" mentioned in the Book of Matthew (6:28)*. The Jerusalem crowfoot, reminiscent of America's buttercup; the sweet-smelling polyanthus narcissus; the pomegranate, noted in Deuteronomy 8; and the almond,

---

*All Biblical quotations in this chapter come from the *Holy Bible*, NRSV, HarperCollins, 1989.

often the first tree to bloom in winter, also contribute to what I heard a Jerusalemite call "the miracle of spring."

Jerusalem: the revered but also defiled cornerstone of the three great monotheistic religions (Judaism, Christianity, and Islam) that trace their ancestry to Abraham of the Old Testament. Emerging from the Judean hills, the city lies east of the Mediterranean Sea and west of the northern tip of the Dead Sea, the lowest point on earth.

This thrice-holy city dates back to the nineteenth century B.C.E. and is mentioned in the Bible 632 times. (In fact, some scholars maintain that the city had human habitation as early as 4000 B.C.E.) In Exodus 3, God refers to the land in which Jerusalem resides as a place "flowing with milk and honey"; yet sadly this land has too often also flowed with blood and tears. Said to have been annihilated at least forty times, the city today remains one of the world's most contested places.

Jerusalem has been known by many names, among them Salem or Shalem in the time of Abraham (2000-1700 B.C.E.), and Zion, the Mountain of God, the City of David; and in the Islamic tradition, it has long been known as Al-Quds ("the Holy"). Perched at 2,630 feet above sea level on the spur of a hill, it is surrounded on all sides by valleys.

The sun rises in Jerusalem over the Mount of Olives and graces first the sacred gold-leafed cupola of the Haram al-Sharif (known in English as the Temple Mount or Mount Moriah, where Abraham nearly sacrificed his son, Isaac). It's a rectangular, eight-gated, tightly walled religious site in the southern part of Jerusalem's Old City—an enclave of less than one square mile in which dwell forty thousand people. As the morning progresses, the sun anoints other Old City monuments, until midday when the sky radiates blue and the sun breathes fire. Sunset brings long shadows and a glow so golden that one almost dares to believe that, indeed, one has reached Jerusalem's fabled "threshold of heaven."

With a recently cited population of about 760,000 residents (two-thirds Jewish, one-third Arab, of whom five percent are Christian), Jerusalem hosts well over two million visitors annually. It first became a pilgrimage destination after the discovery of Christ's tomb in A.D. 326.

By the 1830s, when the Mediterranean could be crossed by steam power rather than sail, the Holy Land (as the followers of Jesus called this Middle East outpost) became a key component of the increasingly popular "Grand Tour." Its appeal as a travel destination continues, although tourism declines during times of violence. Recently, a tour I'd booked suspended all Jerusalem-bound travel because of unrest. Sometime later, when the situation had stabilized, the tour was reinstated and I went.

The city offers far more than physical beauty, I tell my inquiring friends. For many people, a trip to Jerusalem is inspired by religious sentiments. Religious Jews, certainly, are attracted to the Temple Mount, site of the Western Wall, or Wailing Wall, a remnant of their revered Solomon's Temple, also known as "the First Temple" or simply "the Holy Temple."

Solomon's Temple was built c.957 B.C.E. and housed the Ark of the Covenant (the chest containing the two stone tablets inscribed with the Ten Commandments). According to traditional Jewish belief, Solomon's Temple also served as the figurative footstool of God's presence in the tangible world. It was the center of ancient Judaism.

In 587 B.C.E. the Babylonians captured Jerusalem and destroyed Solomon's Temple. It was rebuilt in 516 B.C.E., and became known as "the Second Temple." In about 20 B.C.E., Herod the Great enlarged the Second Temple, also known as Herod's Temple. Ninety years later the Romans destroyed it once again and all that remained was the western wall of the Temple Mount complex. This site then lay in ruin, even becoming a rubbish dump at one point. In A.D. 691, conquering Muslim forces, wanting a shrine to Islam in the Holy City, built the Dome of the Rock on the abandoned Temple Mount platform. They named the site Haram al-Sharif, which in Arabic means "Noble Sanctuary." Since then the Dome of the Rock has dominated Jerusalem and in the eyes of many become its symbol.

Jerusalem has been honored since before the time of Abraham. The Talmud says that the Temple Mount in Jerusalem is home to the Foundation Stone [the name of the rock at the center of the Dome of the Rock], from which some say the world was created.

Through the ages other attempts have been launched to rebuild the Temple, but all have proved fruitless. Jews speak of someday building a Third Temple, but since two Islamic shrines—the Dome of the Rock and the El-Aqsa Mosque, established in A.D. 685—now rest on the Temple Mount platform, this seems an unlikely prospect.

For Christians, Jerusalem's greatest significance lies with Jesus, who came to Jerusalem soon after his birth and made annual visits subsequently.

During one of his visits as an adult, Jesus cleansed the Second Temple of money changers, shouting, "Take these things out of here! Stop making my Father's house a marketplace!" [John 2: 16]. Some time later, just steps from this setting, came the gripping events of Golgotha, the Hill of Calvary, the site of the crucifixion and the events that laid the bedrock for a new faith.

And for Muslims the attachment to Jerusalem stems mainly from Mohammed's miraculous night journey when he is said to have been transported from Mecca to the Temple Mount and from there to heaven and the presence of God, before he was returned to Mecca in the morning. According to Islamic tradition, after Mecca and Medina [in today's Saudi Arabia],

Jerusalem is the third holiest city. For approximately a year, before it was permanently switched to the Ka'ba in Mecca, the *qiblah* for Muslims pointed toward Jerusalem. The city's lasting place in Islam, however, derives from Mohammed's miraculous night journey, or Night of Ascension (c. A.D. 620), an event referred to in Arabic as the *Mi'raj*. (Islamic scholarship suggests that this was a visionary experience, not a physical one.)

Visitors to Jerusalem who are not spiritually motivated might well be prompted by a desire to better understand the region's history, archaeology, democracy, and politics. Jerusalem is many things to many people. To me, it's about physical beauty, but even more, Jerusalem is about its three great religious traditions and its people, who for millennia have been swept up in a great and often terrifying drama—all in the name of the spirit. They have survived in a place that has been both sublimely glorified and grievously desecrated.

Jerusalem has captured my deep and abiding respect and whetted my thirst for yet another visit.

Twice I've had the pleasure of staying at the famed American Colony Hotel in East Jerusalem, the Palestinian Arab part of the city. Once a pasha's palace, in 1902 it began accommodating Western travelers looking for high standards of luxury and service. In time it became a full-fledged boutique hotel, located just beyond the Old City's walls, owned not by Arabs or Jews but jointly by Americans, Britons and Swedes.

The hotel acquired its name as the indirect result of a family tragedy. In 1873, Horatio Spafford, a successful Chicago lawyer and his wife, Anna, both devoutly Christian, lost four daughters in a shipwreck. Five years later their only son died of scarlet fever. Devastated, the Spaffords, along with their two remaining daughters, Bertha and Anna, decided to give up the comforts of Chicago and move to Turkish-controlled Jerusalem to follow in the footsteps of Jesus, offering aid to those in distress. Sixteen Chicago friends joined them, and the group was called by Jerusalemites "the American Colony," a name that lives on.

Initially, the American colonists established themselves inside the Old City near the Damascus Gate, a distinctly Arab neighborhood. Although not formal missionaries, they soon became known for their benevolence: nursing the sick, teaching local mothers about hygiene and nutrition, and offering English and Bible classes.

After Horatio Spafford died of malaria, the colony floundered, but was saved when a group of Swedish families with similar values joined them.* Together this group bought the pasha's palace outside the city walls, which then became a self-sufficient communal entity. Here they planted their own crops and kept their own livestock. They provided their own dressmakers, shoemakers, carpenters, and blacksmiths. Early Zionists made note of their methods, some of which were incorporated in Israel's kibbutz movement.

With the advent of World War I, the colony disintegrated but the hotel survived, remaining in the Spafford family. [Today it is still owned by Spafford descendents, but actively managed by Gauer Hotels of Switzerland.] Surviving heirs have continued their family's charitable ways, most notably in the Spafford Children's Centre, which provides healthcare for thousands of disadvantaged children in Jerusalem in the original Spafford house that abuts the Old City walls.

Historical Jerusalem is readily walkable; distances are short. One morning my traveling companions, fellow Seattleites Jane and Philip, invited me to join them and their goddaughter, Dara, a visiting professor at one of Jerusalem's universities, on a

---

*Seventy Swedes arrived in 1894, followed by fifty-five more in 1896.

walking tour of the Old City.

It consists of four distinct quarters, one each for the Jews, Christians, Muslims, and Armenians.* While the Old City occupies a small geographic area, its population density and irregular terrain can make it a puzzling place to explore—at least at first.

Dara never discussed her own religious affiliation, although from Jane and Philip I knew she had grown up in a Christian home. She did, however, convey a well-rounded understanding of all three Abrahamic faiths. During our walking tour, she reminded us that not every Arab is Muslim—worldwide about fifteen million Arabs are Christians, a fact I had forgotten. In Israel, Palestinian Christians number between forty thousand and ninety thousand. "Most Palestinian Christians belong to the Greek Orthodox Church of Jerusalem," Dara said, adding as an afterthought, "The Roman Catholic denomination here in Jerusalem may now actually outnumber them."

We left the American Colony Hotel from the main portal, heading south, passing first on our right St. George's Cathedral on Nablus Road, an Anglican church built in 1898. "It's part of this country's colonial past," Dara said, pointing to the walled compound in tan stones. "The 1917 truce authorizing the British presence in Palestine was signed in the bishop's quarters," she added, alluding to this land's long history of occupiers. I was struck by the sharp contrast between the cathedral's tranquil setting and the bustling streets of the old Arab neighborhood

---

*The Armenians comprise a nation and ethnic group originating in the Caucasus and in the Armenian Highlands. They number about ten million globally. In A.D. 301, Armenia adopted Christianity as a state religion, becoming the first nation to do so. Its church exists independently of both the Catholic and Eastern Orthodox churches, having become so in A.D. 451 as a result of its excommunication by the Council of Chalcedon. [http://en.wikipedia.org/wiki/Armenians]

surrounding it.

To our left, on Sultan Suleiman Street, lay the Rockefeller Museum, housing important regional archaeological discoveries unearthed since the nineteenth century. Funded by the philanthropist John D. Rockefeller, Jr., it opened in 1938. Dara reminded us that like so many structures in Jerusalem, the Rockefeller Museum has served more than one purpose: "After the building fell into Israeli hands during the 1967 War, its hexagonal tower became a lookout," she said, adding that bitter fighting ensued between Israeli and Jordanian forces, ending in an Israeli victory and the occupation of East Jerusalem.

She directed our attention to the well-visited Garden Tomb, considered by some to be the site of the burial and later resurrection of Jesus Christ. "Now, however," Dara said, "archaeologists lean more toward the theory that the Church of the Holy Sepulchre commemorates that series of events."

After we passed through Damascus Gate, the largest of the seven open gates leading into Jerusalem's enclosed Old City, we found ourselves in the Muslim Quarter, a thousand-year-old network of alleyways first settled by Islamic pilgrims and others resting while en route to Mecca. Today these narrow passageways swarm with life, offering a cacophony of ancient sights and sounds for which the Old City is justly famous: Men in the *keffiyeh*—the shawl-like headcovering held in place by an *agal*—and women in the Islamic headdress moved in easy rhythm alongside us. From eating nooks, the aromas of cardamom, cloves, and cumin wafted toward us. Occasionally, flower-potted geraniums, marigolds, and jasmine saluted us from windowsills that face interior courtyards, offering the privacy valued by Muslims.

Muezzins from nearby mosques honor the ancient five times-a-day call to prayer with "*Allah ... u akbar*," [God is great!]. In the distance, Christian bells chime.

142

Dara led us first to Via Dolorosa, the Way of Sorrows, which tradition suggests follows the route that Jesus took to the cross. We paused at the initial nine Stations of the Cross, sites associated with events believed to have occurred as Jesus struggled toward his crucifixion. At Station VI, for example, Veronica wiped the face of Jesus, at Station VII Jesus fell for the second time, weakened by the flogging he had endured.

As we walked, throngs of people surrounded us—mainly Christian pilgrims, some of whom, in an attempt to replicate the suffering of Jesus, carried heavy wooden crosses on their shoulders.

Although the Way of Sorrows begins in the Muslim Quarter of the Old City, it ends in the Christian and Armenian Quarter at the Church of the Holy Sepulchre, which Dara said serves as the headquarters of the Greek Orthodox Patriarch of Jerusalem. The last five Stations of the Cross are located within the Holy Sepulchre, built over Calvary (Golgotha). It's the most visited part of the Old City, receiving the greatest influx of pilgrims during Holy Week.

The altar of one of the two chapels on Calvary is positioned over a rocky outcrop that is believed to be the actual site of the crucifixion. On the day we visited, the altar was surrounded by prayerful pilgrims, some kneeling and reciting the rosary, others in worshipful repose, seemingly meditating on Christ's suffering: the nailing to the cross, the crown of thorns, the bleeding from five wounds, the cry of agony, *Eloi, Eloi, lema sabachthani?* [My God, my God, why have you forsaken me?] [Mark 15:34], and the final surrender—all to redeem humanity.

As we withdrew from these solemn premises, Philip asked Dara why Golgotha was named the Place of the Skull.

"The word *Golgotha* in Aramaic means 'skull,'" she said. "It's thought that the place we now call Golgotha was once a Roman place of execution where skulls from earlier victims lay scattered about."

Our next stop within the Holy Sepulchre was Christ's Tomb, which Dara said is the holiest place in Christendom. According to the Bible, Joseph of Arimathea owned the crypt and donated it for Jesus' final resting place.

Upon learning of Jesus' death, Joseph of Arimathea went to Pontius Pilate (the Roman governor of Judea from A.D. 26-36, who presided over the trial of Jesus and ordered his crucifixion) to ask for Jesus' body. After receiving it he, along with Nicodemus, prepared it for burial. The two men then carried the wrapped remains to the crypt, and placed them on a large stone in the presence of Mary the mother of Jesus, Mary Magdalene, and other women. Their last act was to seal the tomb by rolling a large, disk-shaped boulder across its entrance. They then departed. What followed, to everyone's initial disbelief, was the resurrection, the core event of Christian doctrine and theology.

As we made our way through the various stations of the Holy Sepulchre, Dara digressed to tell us of the role that Helena of Constantinople (c. A.D. 250-c. A.D. 330), mother of Emperor Constantine, had played in finding early Christian relics. "Traditionally, it's Helena who is credited with unearthing what is believed to be the True Cross, the site of Golgotha, the tomb of Joseph of Arimathea, and the eventual construction of the Church of the Holy Sepulchre."

She said that Helena had been born as an innkeeper's daughter in a Roman province in Asia Minor. In A. D. 270 she married Constantius Chlorus, a Roman general. Two years later she gave birth to Constantine, her only son, who in A.D. 306 became Emperor of the Roman Empire.

In A.D. 293, Emperor Diocletian ordered Constantius Chlorus to divorce Helena and marry a woman named Theodora, apparently a more suitable consort for a man in high office—at least in the eyes of Diocletian.

Helena never married again. She lived a quiet Christian life until A.D. 306 when her son was proclaimed Emperor of the Roman Empire. She then returned to public life, later gaining such titles as Saint Helena, Helena Augusta, Nobilissima Femina, and Helena of Constantinople. She is revered in the Roman Catholic, Orthodox, and Lutheran churches.

In A.D. 325, soon after Christianity was declared legal in the Roman Empire following the Edict of Milan in A.D. 312, Constantine, a newly minted convert, sent his mother to Jerusalem in search of Christian relics. Jerusalem was in disarray, still rebuilding from earlier destructions. As Helena scouted around the city, she found that a previous emperor had built a temple to Venus over what was believed to be the tomb of Jesus.

Legend holds that after walking through this pagan temple, Helena ordered it demolished. She then insisted that it be excavated, which led to the discovery of three crosses, Calvary, and Jesus' tomb. To test their authenticity, Helena brought a dying woman to Golgotha to place her hands upon one of them. Miraculously, the woman was healed. Helena took that as a sign that the cross the woman had touched was indeed the True Cross. To commemorate this site's importance to Christian history, Helena and her emperor son built the Church of the Holy Sepulchre.

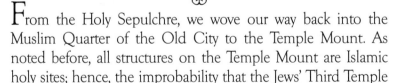

From the Holy Sepulchre, we wove our way back into the Muslim Quarter of the Old City to the Temple Mount. As noted before, all structures on the Temple Mount are Islamic holy sites; hence, the improbability that the Jews' Third Temple will ever be built there.

As we stood gazing at the expansive platform, Dara explained that of the four walls surrounding the Temple Mount, the Western Wall was closest to the venerated Jewish Temples, which once housed the Ark of the Covenant. "For religious Jews," she said, "this site continues to carry a profound aura of holiness." When Philip asked her to amplify that remark, she said that some believers say that all of God's bounty emanated from this spot. Some go so far as to say that it's from this site that God gathered the dust to create the first man, Adam. They also say that to pray here—even today—is to pray before the throne of God. It is the holiest shrine of the Jewish world, revered as the last remnant of the Second Temple.

It was late morning when we approached the Western Wall, where a sign in English and Hebrew greeted us:

Dear Visitors: You are approaching the holy site of the Western Wall where the Divine Presence always rests. Please make sure you are appropriately and modestly dressed so as not to cause harm to this holy place or to the feelings of the worshippers. Sincerely, Rabbi of the Western Wall and Holy Sites.

After passing through security, much like in airports, we crossed a large plaza; at the far end, towering fifty feet above us, the Western Wall loomed, built of massive honey-colored boulders that are said to weigh between two to eight tons each.

My guidebook described the plaza with its imposing wall as a big open-air synagogue, with all of an Orthodox synagogue's strictures: Men and women worship in separate spaces; heads are covered. The morning we were there, the area thronged with black-hatted worshipers of the Hasidic sect, many rocking in prayerful reverie.

Once face-to-face with the wall itself, I saw that, as on previous visits, the gaps between the boulders were filled with small, folded pieces of paper. Tradition holds that petitions left in the crevices of this wall are heard by God, so in keeping with this belief, Jane, Philip, and I stuffed our own prayers into the available spaces.

Dara told us that just a few weeks before his election, Barack Obama had been in Israel to hold meetings with Israeli and Palestinian leaders. In a pre-dawn visit to the Western Wall, he is believed to have inserted between the stones a handwritten prayer, which Dara read to us from her notebook:

Lord: Protect my family and me. Forgive me my sins, and help me guard against pride and despair. Give me the wisdom to do what is right and just. And make me an instrument of your will.

When Philip asked how these details came to be known, Dara said that after Mr. Obama left, a Jewish seminary student supposedly removed the prayer from the wall, which somehow found its way to an Israeli newspaper and publication. The rabbi in charge of the Western Wall and Holy Sites criticized the confiscation of the prayer, saying that petitions left there are the concern only of the supplicant and his God.

As we moved away from the Wall and across the plaza, Philip asked Dara about the key differences between Judaism and Christianity.

"Both traditions see the Old Testament as sacred, but they differ in their perception of the messiah," she said. "The Jews still await their messiah, while Christians believe he has already been manifested as Jesus Christ."

Then Philip asked her to comment on the reservations that Jews and Muslims, as monotheists, have about the Holy Trinity as part of Christian theology.

"Christian theology maintains that God is, indeed, one," she said, "but consists of three aspects: the Father, Son, and Holy Spirit. It's the 'three-ness,' the seeming polytheistic nature of the Christian faith, that prompts some Jews and Muslims to ask if Christians are true monotheists. Christians, of course, see themselves as such: worshipers of a single God. I once heard a Christian clergyman explain the subtlety of the Trinity. He used the analogy of water, steam, and ice; all three elements are still intrinsically H_2O, but can manifest in other forms."

As we strolled from the plaza via the ramp leading to the Mughrabi Gate and the Temple Mount platform, Dara reminded us that Muslims revere this site in large part because of Prophet Mohammad's miraculous nocturnal journey. But their reverence also includes the Patriarch Abraham, along with Kings David and Solomon, all of whom have historical relevance to the Temple Mount and are mentioned in the Qur'an.

"We have to remember," she said, "that Christianity and Islam are daughter faiths of Judaism." I recalled that Abraham's wife, Sarah, was unable to conceive. Wanting her husband to have an heir, she offered him her servant, Hagar, who bore Ishmael, associated with the Arabs. Later Sarah did bear a son, Isaac, who is associated with the Jews.

"Abraham is the progenitor of nearly a billion Muslims," Dara said, "along with two billion Christians, and fourteen million Jews. Followers of those faiths share a powerful common heritage."

Jane wondered when Abraham had appeared on the biblical scene. "According to the Old Testament," Dara said, "it's thought that Abraham came from Mesopotamia to Canaan around 2000-1700 B.C.E. He then entered into a covenant with God: In exchange for his acknowledgment of God as the absolute divine being, Abraham would be blessed with many descendents."

"So, it's safe to assume that Abraham actually existed?" Jane asked.

"According to scripture, yes," Dara said.

After posing for pictures around the blue-tiled facade of

the Dome of the Rock, we examined its geometric lines and glittering golden dome. We learned that the dome was first clad in lead, but is now swathed in aluminum, covered with gold leaf funded by the late King Hussein of Jordan (father of HRH Princess Haya mentioned in the Dubai chapter).

Jane pressed Dara on the significance of the building's outer colors. "In Islamic art," Dara said, "blue symbolizes infinity and gold represents knowledge, which in Islam is considered a kind of spiritual food."

On my previous visits to the Temple Mount, non-Muslims could step inside the Dome of the Rock to view the rock itself. But in recent years the Muslim Administrator and Religious Authority of Haram al-Sharif had closed this site to non-Muslims. According to our guide, with this action the Muslim Administrator and Religious Authority hoped to prevent the type of violence that broke out in 2000, when Ariel Sharon, Israel's then-opposition leader, paid a visit to the Haram al-Sharif with a thousand Israeli police, causing Palestinian frustrations to erupt.

The Temple Mount contains still another famous dome— the one atop the El-Aqsa Mosque, today the chief Islamic place of worship in Jerusalem. Its full name, Dara explained, is El-Aqsa, Arabic for "the farthest mosque," and signifies its being located almost seven hundred miles north of Mecca. She added that it's the second oldest mosque in Islam after the Ka'ba in Mecca.

Dara glanced at her watch. "Do you realize it's nearly noon?" she said. Our morning had evaporated. The sun blistered and the light nearly blinded us.

We stopped briefly for coffee and then walked on to still one more Old City site, the Citadel, a commanding bastion near the Jaffa Gate, where excavations have unearthed remains dating back to the second century B.C.E.

149

The Citadel has particular meaning for Christians since some scholars think that it was here that Jesus stood in trial and condemnation before Pontius Pilate (John: 19:1-16). Today this stronghold is occupied by the Tower of David Museum, offering panoramic views of the city, archaeological remains, and exhibitions that trace the city's history. I liked seeing the hologram of the First Temple and a three-dimensional representation of the Second Temple. I was especially pleased to discover that the Citadel houses a copy of the famous Medici-commissioned bronze statue of young King David, by Andrea del Verrocchio, the Florentine painter, sculptor, and architect (1435-1488). The five-foot-high sculpture was a gift from Florence to Jerusalem.

From my schooldays in Florence and my occasional visits to the original statue's permanent home, the National Museum of the Bargello in Florence, I knew that Verrocchio's model for the young King David was probably his handsome young apprentice, Leonardo da Vinci. In fact, Leonardo spent twelve years as Verrocchio's pupil, securing much of the practical training he needed to become a master in his own right. Leonardo's artistic development is supposed to have proceeded at such a pace that Verrocchio once assigned him the task of painting the angel in *Baptism of Christ, Madonna and Child.* Art historians say that Leonardo's angel exceeded all expectations, causing Verrocchio to vow never to paint again.

By now it was time for lunch. Dara suggested a nearby Levantine* restaurant where, the moment we stepped into its confines, the host greeted us with an exuberant "*Marhaba!*" (hello), followed by an even more exuberant "*Ahlan wa Sahlan!*" (welcome).

---

*The traditional cuisine of the Levant region—lands now apportioned into Syria, Lebanon, Jordan and Israel/Palestine—includes generous amounts of olive oil, thyme, and garlic.

Since Dara still wanted to introduce us to an Old City friend of hers, a Palestinian woman gifted in the needle arts, she suggested that we order lunch quickly. Jane chose *Iggit el Na'na' Wa el Baqdounis* (mint and parsley omelette); Philip selected *Samak Mashwi* (Lebanese broiled fish); and Dara and I decided on the restaurant's version of the famed Jerusalem salad, filled with olives, feta, pomegranates with *za'atar* (a blend of herbs, sesame seeds and salt) sprinkled over it.

Throughout our meal, our host hovered over us like a doting parent. "I have relatives in Detroit—Arab-Americans," he said with delight. When we left he sent us off with high-spirited *ma'a ssalamas* (goodbyes), adding with a twinkle and in English, "Come soon again!"

❀

After lunch, we returned to the Old City to see examples of the famous Palestinian needlework—handcrafted pieces, often with intricate embroidery—art forms now displayed in museums around the world. Such compositions are believed to trace back to the ancient Egyptians, Romans, and Byzantines—all one-time occupiers of Palestine. I was fascinated to learn that age-old Palestinian costumes were so homegrown that they usually defined a woman's marital and economic status, along with her probable place of origin.

"Usually the type of fabric, cut, and embroidery motifs were dead giveaways," Dara said, going on to explain that sometimes communities believed that certain motifs such as triangles, squares, and rosettes were particularly effective in fending off the "evil eye," a common Middle East superstition. To avoid potential curses from envious onlookers, defects were sometimes deliberately embroidered into garments to divert the attention of those gazing.

"Many Palestinian women today have adopted a Western

style of dress," she said, "but some deliberately wear traditional costumes to show respect for their cultural legacy—perhaps not all the time, but on special occasions."

I'd noticed that the basic garment seemed to be a loose-fitting, A-shaped robe with long sleeves.

"Yes," Dara said. "It's called a *thob*, with a chest panel known as the *qabbeh* that often bears the tell-tale motifs of which we just spoke—usually in embroidery. A well crafted *qabbeh* sometimes becomes a family heirloom, passed from mother to daughter."

I asked about the typical colors used in Palestinian heirloom embroidery. "That depended on the materials available for the production of dyes," Dara said. "Red, for example, came from insects and pomegranates, dark blues from the indigo plant, yellow from saffron flowers, and brown from oak bark."

Did Jerusalem have a costume style of its own? I wondered. "Actually no," said Dara. "Jerusalem has always had a multi-ethnic population. People here tend to go with what's trendy, both regionally and internationally. That's what I've liked about living in Jerusalem—its diversity. It's a melting pot. But if you pressed me to suggest nearby Palestinian communities that might have influenced local dress, I'd have to name Bethlehem and Ramallah."

"How were they distinctive?"

"Ramallah women liked white linen for fancy dresses and scarves, but for winter they preferred indigo-dyed linen. Their typical embroidery was a red cross-stitch in silk thread, which contrasted beautifully with the white linen." Bethlehem, she continued, liked to apply gold or silver cords to cloth in unique designs that came to be known as *shughl talhami* [Bethlehem work].

"My friend Em Umar, who is especially gifted in the needle arts, lives in this neighborhood. Among Palestinian women, these artistic expressions are an important cottage industry—with it they help preserve their heritage while also adding some income for their families."

Em Umar greeted us warmly. She wore the traditional Muslim headdress. Dara explained in Arabic who we were and asked to see her creations.

Stacked around Em Umar's work area, we saw an array of traditional Palestinian dresses, all richly embroidered. We also saw piles of pillow covers, shawls, pencil cases, and bags—all in vibrant colors. For several minutes our eyes feasted on the many choices and then, in my case, my gaze rested on a taupe neckscarf, made of cotton, with green and salmon-colored embroidered squares, flower petals, and what I wanted to believe were four-leaf clovers, symbols of good luck. I bought several other pieces from her, mainly those that could be made into pillow cases or wall hangings.

The next morning we taxied across modern Jerusalem to the foot of Mount Herzl, where in 1953 Israel established Yad Vashem, a complex of museums, archives, monuments and sculptures interlocked by a series of walkways designed to commemorate those who died in the Nazi Holocaust. Jane, Philip, and I had visited this memorial on previous trips to Jerusalem and found it to be a deeply moving experience, but never before had the three of us met a Holocaust survivor. On this day we would hear a Jewish grandmother—once an Amsterdam friend of Anne Frank, with whom she had spent part of her teen years in a Nazi concentration camp—tell her story.

We arrived at Yad Vashem early, and used the time before the lecture to reacquaint ourselves with the sprawling campus. While walking through various outdoor commemorative sites, we came across Janusz Korczak Square, where our eyes locked onto a statue of Dr. Henrik Goldschmidt (better known by his pen name Janusz Korczak), the Polish-Jewish children's author, humanitarian, pediatrician, and pedagogue. In this statue Korczak stands in the middle of a group of desolate children, embracing them with strong, outstretched arms, which conveys his powerful resolve to protect them at any cost. The bronze sculpture by Boris Saktsier is called *Janusz Korczak and the Children* and was donated by Mila Brenner and Yakov Meridor.

Dara gave us some background: In 1940, when the Nazis established the Warsaw Ghetto, the Krochmalna Street orphanage, in which Korczak worked, was ordered into the ghetto. Although offered sanctuary among Warsaw's Aryans, Korczak refused, saying simply that he would not abandon his children. Resolutely, he moved into the ghetto with them. On August 5, 1942 the Nazis raided the ghetto, rounding up the orphans for the grizzly one-way trip to Treblinka, a notorious Nazi death camp. Again, Korczak was offered a way out, but again, he declined, saying only that he would go where the children went. For the journey to Treblinka, he dressed the little ones in their finest, and each carried a rucksack, containing a favorite book or toy.

A legend holds that at the point of deportation, an SS officer recognized Korczak as the author of one of his favorite childhood books and tendered an offer for "special treatment"— perhaps at a camp-ghetto like Theresienstadt, where prominent Jews with international reputations were occasionally sent. Once again Korczak is said to have refused. With head held high, along with his nearly two hundred children, he stepped onto the train and into oblivion. No one ever heard from him again. A few children survived, and as adults attended memorials honoring their benefactor.

Our Yad Vashem guest lecturer, Hannah Pick-Goslar,* (known in Anne Frank's diary by the German/Dutch name of "Lies," [diminutive of Elizabeth and pronounced LEES], who spoke fluent but accented English, described growing up in Amsterdam's Jewish community. One day word went around their neighborhood that the Franks had escaped to Switzerland. A sense of relief swept across those who had not been so lucky—that at least a few of their brethren had reached safety. Those left behind carried on bravely, until they, too, were herded together by Nazi guards and deported—in the case of our speaker, to Bergen Belsen concentration camp.

Once in the camp, Hannah learned through the grapevine that Anne Frank was incarcerated there as well. "This can't be!" Hannah cried in disbelief. "She's in Switzerland." But later that night, under relentless searchlight scrutiny, Hannah crept to a predetermined site along a barbed wire fence and saw for herself that her childhood friend, Anne Frank, now an emaciated apparition, was indeed a fellow Bergen Belsen inmate.

"How is it that you're here?" Hannah wailed at the shrunken figure before her. "We thought you'd escaped to Switzerland."

Anne explained that she and her family had gone into hiding, and, as cover, let word go out that they had made their way to safety.

Anne appeared at death's door. Still, wanting to lend a hand—however feeble—to her old friend, now a shell of a human being, Hannah told Anne that over the course of the next day she would scrounge together a few scraps of food and bring them to her on the next night.

At great personal risk, Hannah once again trekked to the appointed place, and after making voice contact with her friend,

---

*Hannah-Pick Goslar's full story is told in the book *Memories of Anne Frank: Reflections of a Childhood Friend* by Alison Leslie Gold.

Hannah threw a small package of rations over the fence to Anne, hoping that this gesture would somehow prolong her life. But before Anne could grab the provisions, a stronger prisoner, hovering nearby, snatched them from midair. On the next night Hannah again made her way to the appointed site. This time, she successfully threw a few morsels over the fence and into Anne's hands. From her voice, Hannah could tell that Anne was joyous. A third reunion was out of the question. Nazi patrols were relentless; punishments brutal. Tragically, soon thereafter Hannah heard that Anne had died of typhus.

Obviously, Hannah survived the ordeal of being reduced to naked subsistence. Anne Frank's father, Otto Frank, survived too. After the war he helped this teenager make her way to Palestine, where she was educated and married, building a productive new life. Now she described her life as that of a devoted grandmother, who occasionally gives public testimonials lest we forget.

The afternoon had been harrowing—a tortuous reminder of man's capacity for hatred, juxtaposed with powerful examples of human goodness. On the way back to our hotel, I thought about how some people were able to withstand death camp horrors and others, sadly, not. Were there any kernels of truth in Nietzsche's famous quote, "He who has a *why* to live can bear almost any *how*"?

The Viennese psychiatrist and Auschwitz survivor Viktor E. Frankl thinks there were. In his acclaimed book *Man's Search for Meaning*, he describes how *love* became his lifeline. Specifically, it was the love for his wife that sustained him. Personally, he had been stripped naked. He had lost every possession. He was cold, hungry, living with the possibility of death at any moment. He didn't even know if his beloved were still alive—they had long ago been separated within the Nazi system of segregation, but through his suffering he came to understand that we can be robbed of everything, except our freedom to choose how we think about a particular situation.

Frankl's riches lay in his mind and spirit. He could still *think*. He could still *feel*. He could still *remember*. He could still *love*. And love he did—dreaming, hoping, and praying for an eventual reunion with his beloved.

Sad to say, when he was liberated he learned that his wife had long ago succumbed. But even in death she had empowered him through the bond of love.

❋

One of my favorite places in Jerusalem is the Mount of Olives [also called Mount Olivet], part of a ridge lying east of the Old City. Its summit offers a breathtaking view across the Kidron Valley to the ancient walled city dominated by the Dome of the Rock.

The Mount of Olives is cited in the Book of Zechariah [14.14] as a place where the dead will be resurrected in the days of the Messiah; hence, Jews have long sought to be buried there, and today the site is estimated to contain about a hundred fifty thousand graves.

At the foot of the Mount of Olives lies the Garden of Gethsemane, one of the most sacred places in the Christian tradition, where Jesus is said to have prayed on the night of his betrayal and arrest.

Visitors at Gethsemane typically walk first among the garden's olive grove, where eight of these gnarled but still fruit-bearing trees are said, but not believed, to be three thousand years old. If not the actual trees to have witnessed Jesus' anguish, some consider them shoots from the trees that did.

During his night of suffering in the Garden of Gethsemane, Jesus prayed while kneeling on a massive rock in the olive grove. [This rock is now enshrined in the Church of All Nations, so named for the twelve countries that funded its construction).

According to Luke 22:42-44, during his agony, Jesus entreated God:

> *"Father, if you are willing, remove this cup from me; yet not my will, but yours be done." Then an angel from heaven appeared to him and gave him strength. In his anguish, he prayed more earnestly, and his sweat became like great drops of blood falling down on the ground.*

The world knows what happened next: Judas kissed Jesus on the cheek, thus identifying him to his persecutors. They arrested him, which led to the crucifixion, burial, and resurrection.

Nestled into the slopes just above Gethsemane, and visible from all over Jerusalem, is the Church of Saint Mary Magdalene, a Russian Orthodox church with seven onion cupolas. It was built in 1888 by Tsar Alexander III (1845-1894), the father of Tsar Nicholas II, the last tsar of Russia, in memory of his mother, Empress Maria Alexandrovna of Russia. When viewed from the Old City, this church brings a touch of whimsy to a hillside otherwise known as a necropolis.

The Sinai Peninsula, a land bridge between Africa and Asia, has been described as twenty-four thousand square miles of nothingness. But it was precisely this nothingness that appealed to people who needed sanctuary, such as Moses, Elijah, Mary and Joseph, along with early Christian radicals. And it was for early Christians seeking refuge in the Sinai that the aforementioned Helena of Constantinople built in A.D. 337 the Chapel of the Virgin where monastic tradition holds that Moses saw the burning bush, from which he heard the voice of God instructing him to lead the Israelites out of Egypt and into Canaan [Exodus: 3:2-6]. Later on Mount Sinai itself: "...[the Lord] gave him the two tablets of the covenant, the tablets of stone, written with the finger of God" [Exodus: 31:18]. The bush that grows there now, a rare rose-family species called *Rubus Sanctus*, is believed to have come from the same stock as the bush from which Moses heard the voice of God. This spiny evergreen is widespread in the Sinai and famous for its longevity.

The Chapel of the Burning Bush eventually evolved into St. Catherine's Monastery, a block-size compound built by Emperor Justinian [A.D. 482-565] between A.D. 527-565 as both fortress and shrine. It is one of the world's oldest continuously functioning Christian monasteries, run by a community of Greek Orthodox monks whose abbot operates under the Greek Orthodox Patriarch of Jerusalem. The monastics dedicate themselves to a life of the spirit through asceticism.

With guidebooks full of lore, Jane, Philip, and I decided to travel from Jerusalem to the Sinai to see for ourselves the monastery [now also a UNESCO World Heritage Site]. We drove first to Eilat, Israel's southernmost town at the northern tip of the Red Sea. There we mingled with dolphins at Dolphin Reef and had dinner in our hotel. After crossing into Egypt the next morning, we were met by our Egyptian guide, Baruti, who escorted us to a beach hotel in Dahab, on the Gulf of Aqaba.

The next afternoon, Baruti drove us to St. Catherine, a hamlet at the foot of Gebel Mûsa, Arabic for "the mountain of Moses," about two hundred air miles from both Jerusalem and Cairo. There he prepared us for our nighttime climb of the legendary 7,455-foot Mount Sinai, following in the footsteps of Moses. "Three thousand seven hundred and fifty steps cut out of stone—a near vertical ascent," Baruti announced grimly. "They are called the Steps of Repentance." To the relief of our little band of senior citizens, Baruti then proposed a more practicable ascent—via a camel trail that switchbacked toward the summit.

When we asked why our climb had to happen at night, Baruti said that sunrise on the Mount is "otherworldly," and besides, by day the sun "paralyzes."

That night our ill-tempered camels, each led by a Bedouin handler, meandered through terrain that by daylight must surely appear as barren and bleak as the face of the moon. The night was cold. Fortunately, we all had jackets.

About three-quarters of the way up the mountain, we dismounted from the camels and climbed the final stretch on foot. While the air chilled us, the world seemed new and fresh. Soon after we reached the summit, hints of light began to signal the dawn. These then melded into distinct bands of pink and blue, slowly touching the granite peaks surrounding the monastery. As I watched darkness turn into light, it seemed as if a genius *Kapellmeister* were orchestrating the metamorphosis.

The Bible does not reveal the exact location of Mount Sinai, and scholars differ over where it is. Tradition places it at Gebel Mûsa in southern Sinai (where we were), but some say that's too far from the Nile Delta for the Israelites to have ventured in Moses' day. These skeptics hold that it might well have been on the far side of the Gulf of Aqaba, in what is Saudi Arabia today.

We came off the mountain around 5 a.m. Baruti then provided us with coffee and we took short siestas in our minibus, before we went to the monastery for its 9 a.m. opening.

The first building we saw in the monastery compound was the Basilica of the Transfiguration, which contains a collection of two thousand icons, some of which are always on view.

Of all the icons I saw that day, the most memorable was *Christ Pantocrator,* where Christ's head is encased in a brilliant golden halo. With his right hand Christ appears to be making the sign of a blessing, and with his left hand he holds a jewel-encrusted

Gospel. Critics comment on his melancholy expression—his mouth is asymmetrical and his eyes are irregular—but to me he exudes an exhilarating authority and strength: The figure seems fully aware of who he is and what he must do. The icon is thought to have been a gift to the monastery by its founder, Emperor Justinian.

Baruti then pointed out the library (tourists are no longer allowed to venture into these guarded premises), which houses forty-five hundred works in Greek, Arabic, Syriac, and Egyptian, including some of the world's most prized religious manuscripts now only viewable on microfilm. "This collection of early Christian manuscripts," he said, "is second only to that found in the Vatican. It's the monastery's most prized possession."

Among the library's treasures is a Charter of Privileges dictated in A.D. 628. by Prophet Mohammed to the monks of the monastery. During the seventh century, when Islamic conquests swept across Egypt and Syria, upheaval followed in its wake. Tradition holds that fearing for the monastery's safety, the monks sent a delegation to Prophet Mohammed asking for protection, which he granted in a letter sent with the returning monks. The letter, which Baruti said can be viewed on the Internet, was essentially an immunity covenant by the Prophet which directed his followers to protect the monks of Sinai from likely danger and destruction.

Tradition further holds that Mohammed actually visited the monastery when he was still a merchant, and perhaps for that reason the monk's petition evoked such a generous response. Perhaps, too, the immunity covenant was a manifestation of Islam's teaching about the *dhimmi,* the protected Peoples of the Book: that Christians and Jews who live among Muslims are not to be harmed.

Baruti then directed us toward the Fatimid Mosque, the Bell Tower, and the Well of Moses, the community's primary source of water. The spiritual heart of the monastery, and for many visitors the highlight, remains the sprawling living bramble that tradition suggests is the offspring of the very bush that Moses saw.

As we made our rounds through the monastery, we glimpsed wary monks who, we suspected, didn't fully approve of the jostling hordes, invading their sacred premises.

Jane wondered why these monks chose to live out here in the wilderness. Baruti said that the emptiness of the desert has long been regarded as a path for spiritual change. He spoke of Moses, John the Baptist, Jesus, and Mohammed, who at various times in their lives deliberately ventured into the wilderness to bask in the silence where they could commune more readily with God. "There they were away from the impieties found in towns. In such simple environments, they believed they could better discern the will of God."

Since the premises were vulnerable to marauders, the monastery was fortified in the sixth century with granite walls sixty feet high and nine feet thick; furthermore, the monks sealed off the outside doors. For most of its existence, the only access to the compound was by a wicker basket that dropped sixty feet to the ground and was then hoisted up again.

"It's mainly monastic tradition that advances the theory that the bush at St. Catherine's Monastery is *the* burning bush," Baruti said. "But tradition can carry heavy weight. Here in southern Sinai, we like to remind ourselves that what matters is that the event happened, not precisely where." He then smiled, adding, "I'm happy you're here and not in Saudi."

❀

Having completed our tour of St. Catherine's Monastery, we drove north toward Cairo, eventually passing under the Suez Canal. As we rolled along Egyptian highways, Jane, Philip, and I fell into conversation about the religious landscape we had traversed the last few weeks—in particular the sacred art we had seen. We pondered the relationship between art and religion.

Philip offered that in his view "Art does not become sacred because of its subject matter, but rather by the expanded consciousness it can induce, maybe a glimpse of the divine."

To that Jane responded, "Well and good, but glimpsing the divine is not enough. It must be made tangible through good deeds—through compassion—for those less well off than we."

Our discussion continued as we drove north toward Cairo in spite of the intense desert heat. In the end we agreed that, indeed, sacred art can be viewed as a means of elevating the heart and mind to a higher reality, but that this is not enough. The higher reality must be transmuted into acts of charity and justice for the least among us. We concluded that even sacred places such as Jerusalem cannot be deemed "sacred" unless they, too, demonstrate charity and justice toward all.

My own thoughts were that I hoped Jerusalem would come to embody these lofty aspirations, and through them move ever closer to lasting peace.

7
Two Baltic Sea Cities:

St. Petersburg & Stockholm

Serendipitously, a Baltic Sea cruise with college alumni brought these two alluring cities my way. Thus, along with enjoying unforgettable shore visits in the present, we could also reminisce and evoke our friendships from long ago. This dual aspect of an early summer sea voyage made memorable the singular beauty and brave history of St. Petersburg and Stockholm.

❀

We were twelve Virginia college alums (from various classes in the 1950s and 1960s), most of whom lived in the southeastern United States; I, the Seattleite, was the outlier. My cabinmate was Elizabeth, an old friend, who divides her time between New Jersey and the Tidewater area. We had all flown into St. Petersburg's Pulkovo Airport from our respective U.S. homes and were now to board an ocean-going French vessel, anchored in a waterway leading to the Gulf of Finland. Our crew was French; our food was French; we were all Americans, but afloat in Russia. A nice mix.

i) St. Petersburg

Sankt Pieter Burkh

Piter

"St. Petersburg is Russian—but it is not Russia."
—Nicholas II, the last Czar

We arrived in St. Petersburg on June 21, the first day of summer, the longest day of the year. It was midpoint in a season Petersburgers call the "White Nights" *(Beliye Nochi)*, when the sun never sets in this city that is often called the "Venice of the North." (St. Petersburg lies just five hundred miles south of the Arctic Circle.) The White Nights peak from June 11 to July 2 and bring with them a celebratory atmosphere not known the rest of the year. Spring has become summer and the earth has turned green. On clear days the clouds frolic in the sky, and the River Neva, the greatest of St. Peterburg's sixty-some tributaries of the Baltic Sea, sparkles as if bedecked with diamonds. Never far from the minds of Peterburgers, however, is the knowledge of how transitory summer can be compared to the long winter nights that await them. (Here it snows from September to May, and the Neva is frozen for at least four months of the year.) Still, for a few joyous weeks of the White Nights, the city pulsates with life. It's not uncommon to find Petersburgers luxuriating in the midnight sun, strolling the night away along their city's watercourses, boulevards, and lilac-filled parks.

On our first evening in this majestic town, a few of my cruise companions and I, along with Vadim, our local guide, joined the throngs. Even as midnight approached, I could see shimmering in the distance the gilded needle of the Cathedral of SS Peter and Paul, where the tombs of the Romanov monarchs rest. Equally luminous was the golden dome of St. Isaac's Cathedral, which, during the Soviet era, bore the name "the museum of atheism."

As we passed what was once the Russian tsars' Winter Palace, but is now part of the Hermitage Museum complex, Vadim described the city's founding in 1703, upon fever-infested swamps that required the labor of forty thousand annually conscripted, often shackled, serfs. Their misery enabled St. Petersburg to become the opulent capital of Europe's most powerful empire, readily compared in its day not only with Venice, but also Amsterdam and Paris. Vadim spoke of the city's three politically induced name changes (Petrograd, 1914; Leningrad, 1924; St. Petersburg, 1991; and its four major revolutions, 1825, 1861, 1905, and 1917.) He grew pensive when he touched on the city's suffering brought on by serfdom, its experiment with Communism, and the gruesome 872-day Nazi siege. "But today," Vadim said, "St. Petersburg is an important trading gateway for Russia's oil and gas exports, shipbuilding, aerospace, electronics, software, and computers." He added that statistics published nearly a decade into the new century report that the Russian mortgage industry issued twenty billion dollars in home loans and expects to quintuple this number within five years. Thirty-six million vehicles were registered around this time, while in 1995 there were a mere eleven million. A struggling graduate student earning spending money as a tour guide, Vadim noted with some irony that Russia has amassed about one hundred nineteen thousand millionaires and fifty-three billionaires.

❋

St. Petersburg exists because of one man—Peter the Great, Tsar of All the Russias [1682-1725], who on May 27, 1703, founded what he initially called "Sankt Pieter Burkh," in honor of his apostolic patron saint.

By 1712, Peter had made his city the capital of the Russian empire, which spanned continents and multiple time zones. By the time he died in 1725, Peter's new port city had forty thousand inhabitants and was set to become a major seafaring power like Holland, a country the young tsar admired.

One of contemporary St. Petersburg's most cherished tributes to Peter the Great is the equestrian statue nicknamed by the poet Alexander Pushkin *The Bronze Horseman*, which shows the city's determined founder mounted on a rearing steed. We visited him on the morning of our first full day in the city. Situated on Decembrist Square, overlooking the Neva River, it's within easy walking distance of the Hermitage Museum.

In 1766, Catherine the Great [1729-1796] commissioned the famous French Rococo sculptor Étienne Maurice Falconet [1716-1791] to create this monument. Catherine was a minor German princess who married into Russia's imperial family. After assuming the throne in 1762, she wanted to affirm her place among Russian monarchs; hence the inscription on the statue in Latin and Russian: *Petro Primo Caterina Secunda* [to Peter the First from Catherine the Second]. She unveiled the statue on the centenary of Peter's accession to the throne, August 7, 1782.

Since Peter the Great had lived in Holland, Britain, and other bustling European centers as a youth, he coveted for Russia, then still mired in superstition and backwardness, the modernizing forces at play in sixteenth-and seventeenth-century Europe.

Falconet presents the Tsar and his steed rearing up from a three-million-pound, thirty-foot-high boulder hauled from Finland and honed to look like a cliff. From this granite precipice, he appears ready to leap into what he believed to be Russia's great future. But just as Peter is about to make his move, his horse steps on a serpent, which causes it to rear up. Vadim argued that the serpent represents the treasonous elements that Peter faced while pursuing his radical venture. In spite of his challenges, the young Tsar jumped headlong into a new world, one that encouraged scientific inquiry, rational thought, technology, a modern army, navy, and organizations of government, art, and literature.

As we stood gazing at *The Bronze Horseman*, Vadim added that to fulfill the dream for Russia, Peter needed infrastructure, which he could only secure by importing the necessary innovation and expertise from Europe. Throughout history, water has played a central role in transportation. And with overland travel between Europe and Russia then still haphazard, even dangerous, Peter decided that his best option for gaining a reliable "window to Europe" was a port. His venue became the swampland of the Neva River delta, on the eastern shores of the Gulf of Finland on the Baltic Sea, giving him ready access to the sea lanes of Europe.

Before saying a reluctant good-bye that morning to the imposing statue, we were told by Vadim that throughout St. Petersburg's often tumultuous existence, its citizens liked to quote Pushkin's poem *The Bronze Horseman* to explain their capacity to endure: so long as their beloved Bronze Horseman gallops still, they will survive. And survive the statue has—through all the vicissitudes of this brave city's history. During World War II, and the long Nazi siege, for example, the statue was sandbagged and then protected in a wooden structure; it emerged unscathed.

✾

Catherine II had no legitimate right to the throne of Russia, but her ingenious way with people propelled her to power. The poet Pushkin said about her: "Her brilliance blinded, her friendliness attracted, and generosity attached." The French philosopher Voltaire (1694-1778), with whom Catherine the Great corresponded for years, called her "The Star of the North." While she subscribed to the ideals of the Enlightenment, and saw herself as a "philosopher on the throne," she did little to improve the plight of the serfs. "She was an all out despot," Vadim scolded.

The Hermitage Museum, just steps from *The Bronze Horseman*, houses three-and-a-half million artistic/cultural exhibits in five magnificent buildings, among which is the aforementioned iconic three-story, green-and-white Baroque Winter Palace.

"Its only rival is the Louvre in Paris and it would take about nine years to glance even superficially at each of the objects on display in the Museum's thousand rooms," Vadim said. Among its riches, the Hermitage collection contains forty Rubenses, twenty-five Rembrandts, more than twenty Van Dycks, two of the ten or twelve authenticated paintings of Leonardo da Vinci, along with dozens of paintings by Italian Renaissance geniuses such as Botticelli, Fra Angelico, and Fra Filippo Lippi.

The art Peter the Great bought for his personal enjoyment while traveling in Europe formed the base of the collection. Then Catherine the Great and her successors added to Peter's treasures by acquiring entire private collections from European monarchs, aristocrats, and auctions. When Nicholas II, the last tsar, ascended the throne in 1894, he inherited the greatest art collection in Europe.

"The 1917 revolution caused the *Imperial* Hermitage to become the *State* Hermitage," Vadim said. "A few years later the Soviet government nationalized the nation's important private art collections, adding them systematically to the Hermitage. To the dismay of many Russian art lovers, in the late 1920s-early 1930s, the Soviet government sold to foreign buyers more than fifty major works, among them Raphael's *Madonna Alba*."

"When talking about the Hermitage Museum," Vadim said, "it's hard not to bring up the Nazi siege." He recounted how during World War II, from September 8, 1941, to January 27, 1944, Leningrad, as the city was then called, lay encircled and besieged by the German Wehrmacht. Hitler vowed to eliminate St. Petersburg from the face of the earth and ordered his forces to be relentless in their assault, systematically destroying reserves and cutting supply lines.

Leningrad had taken few defensive measures. It had food reserves for only thirty days; fuel for peacetime purposes only; no planes or tanks, and a dearth of weapons with ammunition. In December 1941 alone, some fifty-three thousand people died from starvation; another million perished over the next three years. Still, the city repelled Hitler's onslaught—the Nazis advanced into St. Petersburg's suburbs but had to retreat before they could declare victory.

During the Nazi blockade about a million of the museum's best pieces were exiled, along with their curators, to the Ural Mountains. When the war ended, Petersburgers were relieved to learn that every single exiled object had survived.

"So what happened to the pieces that were not exiled, those that stayed behind?" my cabinmate Elizabeth asked.

"A few brave employees chose to stay in the museum to safeguard the remaining objects against the relentless Nazi onslaught," Vadim said. "They dealt with snow, rain, lack of heat and food, not to mention the constant shelling and bombardment. They burned books and furniture for warmth. They melted snow for drinking water. They ate rats for food. Some were reduced to eating wallpaper paste—anything to fill their stomachs. Many died of starvation."

Vadim told of one woman who wrote: "It is so simple to die. You just begin to lose interest, you lie on the bed, and you never again get up." He said that Piskarevskoe Cemetery on the city's perimeter is full of burial mounds containing the remains of hundreds of thousands of Petersburgers who succumbed, but only after displaying a superhuman will to live.

As to why more wasn't done to help the Petersburgers during the siege, Vadim said that the only supply routes were by air or cars crossing Lake Ladoga when frozen. The Nazis often bombed this route, called the Road of Life, so countless numbers of cars full of people and food supplies fell into the icy void.

As Vadim described the courage of Petersburgers during World War II, I recalled my Seattle neighbor's story of her Russian mother, Sabina, who had married a German businessman in the 1930s and lived with him in Riga, Latvia.

In August 1940, the USSR annexed Latvia, which was soon overtaken by Nazi Germany. The war raged. As a German citizen, Sabina's husband was drafted and deployed into the German war machine. Russian-born Sabina, now also a German citizen by marriage, decided to join the multitudes fleeing Latvia's chaos and take her young daughter (my eventual Seattle neighbor), along with her sister and her sister's children, to safety in Germany.

Sabina decided that their best mode of escape from the strife that surrounded them would be by horse-drawn cart and at night. That way, they could take a few belongings, and provide minimal comfort for the children, all under age four. A cart was found, but the best Sabina could do for a horse was a hugely pregnant one, hardly in condition to undertake a treacherous nocturnal seven-hundred-mile journey through battle fields.

On the night of their departure, Sabina and her sister tucked the children into the cart, covered them with down comforters, and tried to explain their need to be quiet—to be brave. The children were too young, too innocent, to understand the complexities of war, but they listened, wide-eyed, as if, perhaps, they grasped some aspects of their plight. At the time of the family's escape, the land swarmed with hostile forces, Nazis and Soviets, all of whom hated the Latvians. A single peep from a child could give their location away, compromise their escape and cost them their lives.

In a corner of the cart, Sabina had squirreled scraps of food, already then hard to come by. She had scrounged wisps of hay for the horse. Drinking water would have to come from creeks, rivers, and snow.

As they plodded, Sabina walked alongside the horse, guiding it by halter and lead rope, prodding it, praising it, all night long on a course that she had researched in advance: Latvia, Lithuania, Poland, and into Germany. They could hear enemy Soviet forces just kilometers behind them. By day this little band of refugees hid—resting, sleeping, if they could—in unobtrusive roadside shelters. They ate remaining crumbs of food. The horse, awkward from pregnancy, and on icy roads, fell repeatedly, and Sabina and her sister then struggled to help this burdened animal stand upright again. Soon they ran out of food, even out of hay. The children wanted to cry out in desperation, but they didn't. Sabina later told me, "Somehow they understood. All we could feed them was snow, which they accepted as food."

When they reached Germany, the refugees were placed in a work camp, where Sabina labored until the war's end to support herself and her child. After the war, Sabina and her husband divorced and Sabina then spent years working in a German chemical lab. After growing into adulthood, Sabina's daughter made her way to the United States where she met an aerospace engineer, also of Russian extraction. They married and raised a family. Upon retirement, Sabina joined her daughter in the Seattle area where she lived out her days in the warm embrace of a loving family.

❀

Once we reached the Hermitage Museum, Vadim guided us directly to the rooms that house the Italian collection.

I lingered longest by the two Leonardo da Vinci works: *Madonna with a Flower* (known as the *Benois Madonna* 1478-80), and *Madonna and Child* (known as the *Litta Madonna* 1490-91).

In the first painting, the young mother, playing with her child, hands him a four-petalled flower, the traditional symbol of the cross.

In the second painting, a comely mother gazes at her infant as she feeds him. Leonardo seemed to illustrate here the very essence of motherly love. Vadim called our attention to the painting's backdrop—symmetrical windows with mountains behind them, suggesting harmony.

When we reached the collection of Dutch paintings, Vadim lost no time zeroing in on Rembrandt's (1606-69) *The Return of the Prodigal Son* (1666-69), perhaps the most famous painting in the museum. The subject comes from the Gospel According to Luke 15:20-24, in which a son asks his father for his inheritance, leaves home, then wastes away his fortune. Ailing and penniless he returns to his father's house.

The old man forgives him, just as God forgives those who are penitent.

Vadim described Rembrandt as a master storyteller and a master psychologist, and asked us to note the intensity of emotion—remorse, compassion, love and sorrow—in his portrayal of the old, arthritic but kindly parent, and the kneeling son.

"Who actually acquired *Return of the Prodigal Son*? asked David, a retired professor from Charlottesville.

"Catherine the Great. She bought it in 1766, for under six thousand French francs." Vadim told us that Catherine was a passionate and prodigious collector, and is quoted as having said: "I am not an amateur, I am a glutton."

The Hermitage was getting more crowded now, and Vadim moved us along, quickening our pace. We saw the Great Throne Room with its parquet floor made from sixteen types of wood, the Pavilion Hall with its famous golden Peacock Clock, and the gallery of classical antiquity where we ogled the sixth-century Scythian gold stag. As we circulated, Vadim pointed out the painted ceilings, crystal chandeliers, inlaid marquetry, decorative items of jasper, lapis lazuli and amber that some in our group declared surpassed the paintings in splendor.

When we reached the Spanish collection, I learned that the Hermitage owns seventeen works by Murillo, the artist whose painting *El Ángel del la Guarda* I had so enjoyed in the Cathedral of Seville. Here it was Murillo's *Boy with a Dog*—another piece featuring children—that caught my eye.

As we were concluding our visit, David asked, "Vadim, we didn't see much homegrown art here. The collection seems heavily invested in European art. Why is that?"

"To see homegrown art, you'd have to go to the Russian Museum, which specializes in just that. It's housed in the Mikhaylovskiy Palace, a neo-classical creation built from 1819-25. It's not on our itinerary, but you'll have some free time."

"What might we see there?" Elizabeth asked.

"Wonderful Russian folk art—painted ceramics, embroidered tapestries, and lacquered spoons and dishes. A lot of it was made by serf craftsmen on estates before their emancipation in 1861. You'll also see examples of social realism: *The Barge-Haulers on the Volga* (1870-73) by Ilya Repin is a great painting in which the artist expresses his condemnation of forced labor by portraying the great dignity of those who were exploited."

Someone then asked about the institution of serfdom.

"The privileged life of the tsars depended on serfs and peasants," Vadim said. "It wasn't too different from your slavery, at the core of the U.S. economy for two centuries."

Elizabeth brought up a book that contrasts Russian serfdom with American slavery: *The Pearl: A True Tale of Forbidden Love in Catherine the Great's Russia,* by the historian Douglas Smith. He viewed slaves as being in continual dehumanizing and brutal bondage, whereas serfs lived most often at a distance from the owners of the land they were enslaved to farm. Because masters were absentee owners, their charges were free from constant and often repressive oversight. As an aside, Elizabeth mentioned the serf woman Douglas Smith portrays—Praskovia Kovalyova (1768-1803)—who became one of the country's most acclaimed divas and eventually the wife of her master, the richest aristocrat in Catherine the Great's Russia, Count Nicholas Sheremetev (1751-1809).

Vadim thanked Elizabeth for her contribution and said that this illicit relationship was legendary in Russia, especially among the peasantry. "Forbidden love between master and serf was not uncommon, but marriage between these two classes was."

He went on to discuss the post-Emancipation challenge of providing tens of millions of freed people with education and jobs. At this Russia failed miserably, he said. Progress was too slow, and Russia slid toward revolution. We all know the rest of the story, with Russia's decades-long experiment with Communism.

❋

That evening a few from our group took in the ballet, *Swan Lake*, originally choreographed by Julius Reisinger (1827-1892) to the music of Pyotr Ilyich Tchaikovsky (1840-1893). (It was first performed from February 20 to March 4, 1877, as *The Lake of the Swans* by the Ballet of the Moscow Imperial Bolshoi Theatre.).

I had seen *Swan Lake* before, but never a performance that conveyed such deep emotion. When I later mentioned this to Vadim, he said that Russian ballet has a spiritual dimension that is often absent in other interpretations. He cited St. Petersburg's acclaimed daughter, Anna Pavlova (1881-1931), perhaps the greatest ballerina the world has ever known, who gained her initial fame through her performance in *The Dying Swan*. Her special gift as an artist lay in her ability to impart her soul. Where a composer uses instruments to express music or a visual artist uses color and brushes to express a vision or an actor uses words and gestures to convey character, Pavlova used her body and spirit to communicate a language she viewed as universal.

The critic André Levinson (1887-1933) said "She moved as if in prayer," and, in *Giselle*, "as if an angel had come to announce the birth of a Messiah."

❋

Early morning of our second day in St. Petersburg, Vadim bussed us about fifteen miles into the countryside to visit the Catherine Palace at Tsarskoe Selo ("Tsar's Village"). This palatial country retreat was designed in 1752 by the Russian architect of Italian origin, Francesco Bartolomeo Rastrelli (1700-71).

He had developed an easily recognizable style, known as

Russian Baroque, that honored Russia's Eurasian past—the early churches and monasteries of Old Russia—but also included Italian and French Rococo innovations. Adept not only at exterior designs, Rastrelli introduced color, movement, and light to his interiors through the careful placement of windows, mirrors, ceiling frescoes, and parquet floors.

Among his most acclaimed works: the Winter Palace in St. Petersburg and the Catherine Palace in Tsarskoe Selo.

Vadim explained that in the eighteenth century a monarch's power and standing were judged by the splendor of his residences and their interiors. A "Versailles complex" had swept through many of the royal houses of Europe. The Russian monarchs had been particularly susceptible to this mania, believing, indeed, that a nation's imperial power must be reflected in the grandeur of its architecture.

By the 1740s, St. Petersburg had grown into more than the sum of its architectural achievements: It had become a citadel, a thriving port, a doorway to the West, and a governmental stronghold. Peter the Great's dream had come true.

My first glimpse of Catherine's Palace was of its brilliant turquoise facade with white columns and gold statues. We were looking at a fully restored version of a palace that had been severely damaged during World War II, even occupied by Nazi forces during their siege. Rastrelli liked to paint his baroque buildings in over-the-top colors—pink, red, green, yellow, and the just noted turquoise—vibrant colors that would enliven this otherwise bleak, northern land; he liked lavish ornamentation and lots of gilding. Here he indulged all of his desires.

As we approached the palace's main entrance, I looked left, where loomed the imperial chapel with its five golden onion-shaped cupolas.

After entering the palace, we made our way up the white marble Great Staircase, its brilliance offset by wine-red carpeting and window drapes. Vadim said this stairway is a prime example of the Neoclassical style that Catherine the Great preferred.

Now we floated through a series of stately rooms, the most dramatic of which, the Amber Room, has been called the "eighth wonder of the world."

I was nearly mesmerized by the quantities of magnificent inlaid amber (dried resin from prehistoric trees) and its warm hues: every variation of yellow, ranging from shadowy topaz to vivid lemon.

The Amber Room was created in Berlin between 1701 and 1709 for that city's extravagant Charlottenburg Palace, home of Friedrich I (1657-1713), the first king of Prussia. In 1716 Peter the Great, ever the collector of rare European artistic treasures, made an official visit to Prussia's king in Charlottenburg Palace and expressed admiration for the Amber Room (*Bernsteinzimmer* in German). Eager to bolster Prussian-Russian relations, King Frederick Wilhelm I (1688-1740) presented his guest with the magnificent inlaid amber panels. They were transported to Russia by sleigh. Once there, local craftsmen could not reassemble them, and these orange gems, often called "Gold of the North," languished in storage for decades.

In the 1740s, Empress Elizabeth ordered that the panels be installed in St. Petersburg's Winter Palace. In 1755 she changed her mind, instructing that they be moved to her summer residence, Catherine's Palace, where they remained until World War II.

Germany invaded Russia in June of 1941. At breakneck speed, with forces that included four million German soldiers, nearly two hundred divisions, and three thousand tanks, the Wehrmacht bulldozed its way across the Soviet Union. As noted earlier, museum curators managed to spirit some art treasures to safety, but many were left behind, among them the Amber Room. To complicate the crisis, curators who were to secure remaining treasures were unexpectedly reassigned to support municipal defenses. One recorded in her diary: "We carry out the work of guards, office workers, cleaners."

With the Wehrmacht drawing ever closer to Catherine Palace, curators decided that their only recourse was to try to mislead the Nazis by hiding the amber panels *in situ* behind fake walls covered with ordinary wallpaper. But the Nazis found the panels and within thirty-six hours had dismantled them. Soon thereafter they were shipped to Königsberg in East Prussia and displayed for a time. Then they disappeared. Of the many theories about the disappearance, Vadim favored the one that suggests that the Amber Room was probably destroyed in 1944, when Königsberg Castle was bombed in Allied air raids.

"So how did the Amber Room come to be reconstructed?" asked David.

"Full-scale reconstruction began in the 1980s with Russian craftsmen," Vadim said, adding that reference materials for this project consisted mainly of black-and-white photographs and staff recollections. When the Communist government ceased funding the project in the 1990s, donations poured in, including a gift of $3.5 million from the German company Ruhrgas. The restoration consumed about six tons of raw amber and cost about eleven million dollars. The new Amber Room was dedicated in 2003 by President Vladimir Putin and German Chancellor Gerhard Schröder at the three-hundred-year anniversary of the founding of St. Petersburg. Vadim said that some believe the Amber Room symbolizes the long and sometimes trying history of Russian-German relations.

As we strolled toward our bus, we learned that this palace-and-park combination had been the last home of Tsar Nicholas II. After his abdication in 1917, he and his family, along with a few servants, were first held here at Tsarskoe Selo and then transferred to Ekaterinburg where they were executed during the summer of 1918. Their bodies were buried in a nearby forest and not found until 1979. Vadim later took us to the Peter and Paul Cathedral in St. Petersburg, the final resting place of the Romanov monarchs. In a small side chapel, we viewed the tomb of Nicholas II, his wife, their children, and members of their immediate household, whose remains were interred there in 1998. (The Tsar's mother, the Dowager Empress Maria Fedorovna (1847-1928), managed to escape the Revolution to her native Denmark, but in 2006 her remains were brought back to Russia for reburial next to her husband in the Peter and Paul Cathedral.) In 2000, the Russian Orthodox Church canonized the last tsar and his immediate family.

After a sumptuous lunch on our French vessel, and before setting sail for Sweden that evening, Vadim escorted those who were interested to the Nevsky Prospekt, the most famous street in Russia, often compared to the Champs-Elysées.

Nevsky Prospekt was designed by the French architect Alexandre Jean-Baptiste LeBlond (1679-1719) whose creations in France had caught Peter the Great's eye. At the Tsar's invitation, LeBlond arrived in St. Petersburg in 1716 and immediately received the extraordinary title of Architect-General. His task: to lay out St. Petersburg. In 1718, LeBlond's commissions grew to include planning what would become the city's main artery, then a three-mile stretch of dense, wolf-infested forest. In spite of LeBlond's careful design, at least twice between 1721 and 1777 St. Petersburg suffered such severe flooding that his acclaimed thoroughfare, Nevsky Prospekt, became a waterway completely navigable by boat.

Today Nevsky Prospekt represents the heart of St. Petersburg, prized by residents and visitors for its architecture, shopping, entertainment, and nightlife.

As we strolled along Nevsky Prospekt, we crossed canals,

gazed at shops, passed the Grand Hotel Europe, where, Vadim whispered, "the Queen of England slept," until we reached the Literary Café, long the watering hole of St. Petersburg's best and brightest, among them Fyodor Dostoevsky and Alexander Pushkin. Here we paused for coffee.

As I watched a smart, young Russian woman in mini-skirt and sleeveless top (it was June!) nibble at her dish of *morozhenoe* (ice cream), Vadim said that the dull food of the Soviet era had largely been replaced with more traditional cuisine: herring, sturgeon or salmon-laden hors d'oeuvres; *borscht* (red beet and cabbage soup), and when available fresh water fish with dill sauce. "*Bliny* (pancakes) are a favorite, too, and fast-food places have quickly appropriated them as one of their most profitable niches." He went on to say that this delicacy is typically filled with meat, mushroom, egg, cheese and green onions. "It's a food that people can eat on the run." He smiled and added, "We're becoming a nation almost as rushed as you."

While most of our little group drank some kind of coffee beverage, Vadim consumed tea and with it spoonfuls of *varenye* (jam) served on the side. He saw that I was watching him and volunteered, "A lot of us use jam as a tea sweetener. It's a Russian tradition."

"So what type of jam is preferred for this purpose?" I asked.

"I happen to be using raspberry today, but a favorite here in Petersburg is blackcurrant, a berry we gather in our nearby forests."

Vadim then shifted our attention to the fact that in 1837, this café was the very place from which Alexander Pushkin left for his mortal duel with Georges d'Anthès, the cavalry soldier who had for some time made overtures toward Pushkin's wife. D'Anthès shot first, fatally wounding the poet, who died two days later, at the age of thirty-eight.

In spite of his short life, Pushkin had left his mark—not

only as a literary genius, but also as one who dared to ask, "At what price St. Petersburg's glories?" He became an advocate for human rights, pleading for Russia's oppressed. He called for an end to autocracy and campaigned for a constitution.

Pushkin's rhetoric caught fire. Sparks flew. Embers smoldered. Shots rang out. The serfs were freed in 1861 and the Revolution erupted in 1917. Then came decades of suffering and heroism. Throughout the city's three-hundred-year history, Petersburgers have repeatedly shown a resolve to prevail in the face of horrific odds. May they continue in that tradition and be rewarded for their efforts!

ii) Stockholm

"The Northern Star."
—Time (July 4, 2011)

The Swedish writer Selma Lagerlöf, the first woman to win the Nobel Prize in Literature (1909), spoke of Stockholm as "a city that floats on water." Indeed, Stockholm, the capital of Sweden, a country about the size of California, stretches across fourteen islands, draped in greenery and red brick buildings. In June the water surrounding these islands glitters, the light above gives off a brightness that makes one cry out for shade, and flowers, birdsong, and mosquitoes abound, while salmon-stocking programs make the inner-city waterways a fisherman's dream.

Around summer solstice, Stockholm, which lies on the 56th latitude (St. Petersburg is on the 60th), revels in about eighteen hours of daylight. To celebrate this season, pagan traditions are resurrected in spite of a thousand years of Christianity. People decorate maypoles, place flower wreaths on their heads, dance, eat, and drink until the next, much-awaited sunrise when the sky often shimmers robin's-egg blue with streaks in soft pastels.

About five hours before we anchored in Stockholm proper, we began threading our way through the archipelago of fourteen thousand to one hundred thousand forest-filled islands that surround it. As I looked out, and drank in the towering evergreens, wild flowers, jumping fish, and diving gulls, I thought of my own corner of the world and the archipelago of about 457 islands that lie off Seattle's shore: the San Juan Islands (Orcas, Lopez, and Shaw are among them) reachable only by air or sea—ideal for those seeking a simpler life.

Between 1850 to 1920, twenty-five percent of the Swedish population emigrated to the United States. The cause: poverty, but also, in the minds of many, a lack of religious freedom under the Swedish Lutheran state church. Then came the famine of 1867-1868 when crops failed and the choice was to starve or emigrate. Many of these early immigrants settled in Minnesota or on the prairies. Then, by the 1880s, when trains could travel west, a succeeding wave of Swedes journeyed to the West Coast, many to Seattle, a place that surely must have looked to them like home. My late husband's parents were among those Swedish immigrants, having left their native land around 1900 as teenagers, unaware of each other until they settled in Seattle where they met and married. They were among the early arrivals in Washington's Swedish-American community, which today constitutes about 3.6 percent of the state's population.

❁

When our boat anchored in Stockholm, Gabriella met us and for the next two days ferried us around her city. One of the men in our group called her "a Nordic goddess in her prime"; we guessed she was about 45.

First on her agenda was Gamla Stan (Old Town), situated on its own small island. It was here that the city's history began, around 1250, as an encampment for fishermen and hunters.

This early settlement soon grew into a trading post and fort whose purpose was to cordon off the inland waterways from Baltic Sea interlopers. By the seventeenth century Sweden had mushroomed into one of Europe's leading naval powers, with territories throughout the Baltic Sea. For a time Sweden even had a colony in the New World—on the mouth of the Delaware River, where Wilmington stands today—but that was short-lived, soon falling into Dutch hands.

When the industrial revolution arrived at the close of the nineteenth century, Swedes fled by the thousands from their agrarian lives into Stockholm, looking for jobs. Some were able to make a go of it in the city that then consisted of about three hundred thousand inhabitants. Others, lured by the American Homestead Act of 1862, which promised one hundred sixty acres free to anyone who would live on the land and farm it for five years, social freedoms (including religious autonomy), and lower taxes, joined the mass exodus that took one-fourth of Sweden's population to North America. Today greater Stockholm is a thriving metropolis of about two million people, and is Scandinavia's largest city, with the most multinational firms and the biggest stock market.

As we strolled through Gamla Stan, I found a maze of cobblestone lanes; yellow, orange, and red buildings; and old fortified walls sometimes etched with ancient Viking Runestones, written in Old Norse, listing Swedes who had participated in Viking expeditions.

"Our knowledge of the Viking Age [A.D. 800 to 1000]," Gabriella said, "comes mainly from tales left by people who actually met Vikings—English monks, Arab traders in Constantinople, along with accounts Vikings gave of themselves in Icelandic sagas." For centuries Viking stories were transmitted orally; only in the thirteenth and fourteenth centuries did they begin to be recorded. Gabriella described Vikings as skillful boat builders, mariners, warriors, traders, settlers, even poets and story-tellers. Their boats were the fastest ships of the age, with drafts shallow enough for easy beaching, and were readily maneuverable in rivers. Swedish Vikings preferred easterly destinations—crossing the Baltic Sea to Russia, and, occasionally to the Black and Caspian Seas. Their purpose, to trade and plunder. On such expeditions they deployed fully armed with sword, knife, and axe—many never to return again. Unearthed Runestones often pay tribute to a dead family member with the expression, "fed the eagles."

As we walked in the morning light, I saw a hot-air balloon drifting languidly above us. Stockholm is the only world capital that sanctions balloon travel within the city limits. We lingered over coffee, a respite that in Stockholm is called *fika* and is a national fixation. A caffeinated interlude here is best enjoyed with the city's famous *kanelbulle* (cinnamon buns) and with at least one of the country's daily newspapers in hand.

Gabriella shared a favorite local joke about her fellow countrymen: Swedes are so polite that they typically employ the expression "thank you" fifteen times while making a purchase as simple as a newspaper.

Surveying the café's customers absorbed in reading their dailies, Gabriella mentioned that Swedes believe firmly in freedom of expression, a reality that traces back to the Freedom of the Press Act from 1766. "Swedes maintain that the public has a right to be informed and that journalists are society's guardians," she said.

Among the customers were people clearly of other ethnicities, and we learned from Gabriella that since World War II, Sweden has become a major haven for immigrants, lately Iraqis, Somalis, Turks, and Iranians.

At a nearby table, a baby fussed in his stroller. His athletically handsome father then lifted the infant into his arms, and with practiced hands quieted him with juice—a demonstration of how Sweden has become a gender-equality nation where mothers work while fathers assume a fair share of childcare responsibilities.

I wondered aloud about how Swedish women can be so enviably slim while eating pastries like the *kanelbulle*.

"We eat sweets, of course, but in moderation," Gabriella said. "Our slenderness comes from walking and not yet having bought into the junk-food culture. We live on what we produce naturally—fish from the nearby ocean and our lakes (which number about ninety-six thoussnd). Reindeer, venison and elk contribute to our diet, along with vegetables, especially hot boiled potatoes and our crisp bread called Wasabröd."

The super-lean Gabriella, mother of two, confessed that her cholesterol is 130. "And I don't use statins!" she announced proudly.

Stockholm impressed me as a place on the cutting edge of innovation. The city powers its buses with bio-gas and uses rainwater for irrigation. In 2010 it was named Europe's first green capital. Stockholm aspires to be a fossil-fuel-free city by 2050. In the interim, it hopes to export this "outside the box" way of thinking to the world, thus also turning green into gold.

Once we resumed our stroll through Gamla Stan, I was especially interested to see the Royal Palace (*Kungliga Slottet*), the official residence of the Swedish monarch. The private residence of the royal family is Drottningholm Palace, about six miles away from Gamla Stan and easily reachable by boat, underground rail, bus or car.

The Royal Palace is emblematic of an era (1611-1721) when Sweden was one of the most powerful states in the Baltic Sea. For about seventy-two of the above-mentioned years, Sweden was at war, annexing provinces in Denmark and Norway, parts of northern Germany, and all of Finland. Through these conquests, the Swedes acquired and brought home spectacular art treasures that feathered the many newly sprouting palaces. Clearly, the Swedes had bought into the "Versailles Complex" then sweeping the royal houses of Europe: that a nation's power must be reflected in the grandeur of its architecture and interior design.

The site of today's Royal Palace in the eleventh century was nothing more than a defensive installation; by the thirteenth century it had become a fortress; and by the fourteenth century a royal residence, which in time evolved into a Renaissance palace that burned to the ground in 1697. What followed is today's yellow-brown palace that Gabriella described as being in the Roman style with a French interior.

In addition to serving as a royal workplace and the backdrop for official functions, the palace is a museum, housing one-of-a-kind artifacts in a variety of spaces: the State Apartments, the Bernadotte Apartments, the Guest Apartments, the Treasury with the State Regalia, and Sweden's oldest museum, the Royal Armory (1628), which showcases such historical art objects as gilded carriages, even a fully restored coronation carriage.

Sweden is a constitutional monarchy, with King Carl Gustaf XVI (b.1946) currently reigning. The King is essentially a figurehead, performing only ceremonial functions. His consort is Queen Silvia (b.1943), who was born a commoner in Heidelberg, Germany, the city where I grew up after World War II. From 1947 to 1957 her father, Walther Sommerlath, took his family to live in São Paulo, Brazil, eventually returning to Heidelberg in the late 1950s just before I left for college in the United States. Silvia and I never met during our Heidelberg years, but my mother and Silvia's mother, Alice Sommerlath, became friends. Through that association, when Queen Silvia came to Heidelberg to visit her family, my mother was occasionally invited to tea in the Sommerlath home. She described Queen Silvia as beautiful, poised, and kind—always personally serving tea to the assembled guests. Silvia's father died in 1990. When his widow's health failed, Silvia brought her mother to Stockholm, where she was nurtured until her death some years ago. Queen Silvia is a patron of over sixty causes, among them disabled children, dementia and the care of the elderly, particularly those at the end of life.

The present royal family tries to stay close to the people. They sent their children to public schools and take an interest in popular charities. Gabriella said that the affection that most Swedes feel for the royals is the family's best defense against the occasional cries for abolition of the monarchy. Polls show that about seventy-two percent of the people favor the continuation of the monarchy.

❀

In 1926 when architect Ivar Tengbom designed Stockholm's Konserthuset (the Concert Hall), he said that he wanted to "raise a musical temple not far from the Arctic Circle." This he achieved. Annually, Konserthuset offers in its Main Hall some seventy Classical and Romantic concerts by the Swedish Philharmonic Orchestra. Secondarily, Konserthuset provides the venue each December 10 for the Nobel Prize presentations in physics, chemistry, physiology or medicine, economics, and literature. (The Nobel Peace Prize is presented in Oslo's City Hall on the same date.) This celebration is followed by a banquet in the Blue Hall of Stockholm's Stadshuset (City Hall), today considered the symbol of the city.

Before we reached Stadshuset, Gabriella reminded us that Alfred Nobel (1833-96) was a chemist and the inventor of high-explosive dynamite, as well as being the benefactor of the distinguished Nobel Prizes, which the Swedish monarch has presented every year since 1901 on December 10, the anniversary of Nobel's death.

Gabriella speculated that Nobel's motive for creating this prize was to make amends for the damage done by dynamite. He bequeathed ninety-four percent of his assets to establish and endow the five Nobel prizes to be awarded to persons who "shall have conferred the greatest benefit on mankind." As for the Nobel Peace Prize, he wrote in his will that it should honor "the best work for fraternity between nations, for the abolition or reduction of standing armies and for the holding and promotion of peace congresses."

The Stadshuset was built in 1923 along Stockholm's waterfront in a style that some say is reminiscent of an Italian palazzo; others say it looks like nothing more than a big church. Soaring above this structure is a 328-foot square tower that affords a sweeping view of Gamla Stan. While the Stadshuset's Blue Hall is the site of the annual Nobel Prize banquet, I liked best the Golden Hall, one flight above, with its celebrated mosaic walls that depict—via eighteen million gold-leaf tiles—motifs from Swedish history. In this breathtaking room, I felt as if I'd been transported to Ravenna, Italy, where, during my art-history student days, Professor Raffanelli took us to see the stunning mosaics in the Basilica di San Vitale (527-548), prime examples of early Christian/Byzantine art and architecture in Europe.

Wall mosaics were a relatively new art form in the early Christian era. They replaced the older and cheaper medium of mural painting. I recall a Raffanelli lecture in which she said that as Christianity took hold in the early centuries of the first millennium, and new Christian churches multiplied, huge wall surfaces suddenly had to be adorned with images worthy of their structures. Out of this need grew the wall mosaic as an art form, engineered initially through small cubes of marble, and later through cubes of glass that shimmered in deeper and more intense colors than did marble. Gold was a popular color then—"a touch of heaven here on earth," the usually understated Gabriella effused—and the predominant color in Stockholm's majestic Golden Hall.

✿

I first came across Sweden's Royal Warship, the *Vasa*, through the January 1962 *National Geographic*, which featured an article on the ill-fated, top-heavy oak vessel that capsized and sank unexpectedly just fourteen hundred yards into its maiden voyage, on August 10, 1628, killing 50 people. [Sweden's King Gustavus Adolphus had ordered the warship built in tribute to the founder of his dynasty, Gustav Vasa.] After this calamity, the pride of the Swedish fleet languished for more than three hundred years on the bottom of Stockholm Harbor in one hundred ten feet of cold, brackish Baltic Sea waters.

In 1956, a Swedish marine archaeologist's persistent search led to the discovery of the nearly forgotten warship, which was painstakingly raised, towed to a dry dock, and restored to ninety-five percent of its original form. "The hardest part, after the actual salvage," Gabriella said, "was making sense of the twenty-four thousand loose objects that were found in, and later salvaged from, the seabed of thirty-two thousand cubic feet around the relatively intact galleon's hull." These included skeletons, clothing, tools, coins, rum, butter and utensils, which had to be reassembled like a mammoth three-dimensional jigsaw puzzle. Today the reconstructed Vasa, inaugurated in 1990, is Stockholm's most cherished historical relic and most popular tourist destination. Historians today value the Vasa [originally designed as a propaganda tool with sixty-four bronze cannons and four hundred fifty men] not only for her status as the planet's oldest preserved and identified vessel, but also for what it reveals about everyday seventeenth century life. When we asked why the Vasa had not suffered more from decomposition and erosion, Gabriella said that "Shipworms destroy wood in salty waters, and the Baltic Sea lacks the salinity that shipworms need to live."

Upon entering the Vasa Museét (Vasa Museum) that houses the ship, I was first struck by the low light-levels and obvious temperature controls (65° to 68° F) that protect the resurrected ship. We couldn't board the vessel, but we could come close enough to see its richly decorated facade—much of it in vivid colors, even gilded. I liked best the restored figures, sculpted life-size and battle-ready, lining portions of the stern. Some appear in human form, others as ferocious monsters, intended to proclaim the King's power and taunt his foes.

For a country with just fifteen million inhabitants on the northern edge of Europe, Sweden has given the world an impressive array of cultural figures. Among them: the aforementioned Selma Lagerlöf; August Strindberg, playwright and writer; Astrid Lindgren, author and screenwriter, whose many works were translated into eighty-five languages in more than one hundred countries, selling 145 million copies worldwide; and Ingmar Bergman, Greta Garbo, and Ingrid Bergman of celluloid fame, along with ABBA, the popular music group.

Astrid Lindgren wrote *Pippi Longstocking*, a series of renowned children's books whose lead character is the imaginary Pippi, the red-haired, pig-tailed girl with a suitcase full of gold and a tree that flows with chocolate and soda pop.

As we made our rounds through old Stockholm, we came across a startling memorial showing people rising out of cement. Nearby, also in cememt, lay a bronze signature—a copy of Raoul Wallenberg's autograph.

Gabriella explained that this was the "Homage to Raoul

Wallenberg Monument," a memorial created in 2001 and unveiled by Sweden's King Carl Gustaf XVI, in memory of the Swedish humanitarian who helped rescue thousands of Jews from the Holocaust.

"Sweden has a long history of helping to resolve international conflicts," Gabriella continued. She told us that while Sweden aggressively built an empire in the sevententh century, in the early nineteenth century it adopted a policy of neutrality in armed conflicts.

This policy came about through Sweden's role in the Napoleonic Wars, during which over a third of the country's territory was lost, including Finland to Russia. A *coup d'état* ensued. The succeeding regime formulated a new foreign policy—known as *The Policy of 1812*—that Sweden would no longer participate in any armed conflicts. Sweden does, however, engage in global peacekeeping missions. This policy produced such celebrated twentieth-century Swedish peacemakers as Count Folke Bernadotte, who, through artful negotiations with the Nazis, engineered the release of thousands of prisoners from concentration camps; Raoul Wallenberg, who, while first secretary of the Swedish legation in Budapest in 1944, helped many Hungarian Jews flee deportation to Nazi concentration camps; and Dag Hammarskjöld, Swedish diplomat and second Secretary-General of the United Nations (1953-1961), who worked tirelessly to build the U.N.'s stature in the world.

Among Hammarskjöld's achievements was the creation of the UN Peacekeeping Force and the release from China of captured American pilots. In September 1961, on still another peace mission—this time to the Congo—he and fifteen others met their deaths in a plane crash under still unresolved circumstances. Some say he was assassinated.

After his death, President John F. Kennedy described himself as a small man in comparison to Hammarskjöld who he considered as "the greatest statesman of our century." Hammarskjöld was awarded the Nobel Peace Prize posthumously.

Afterword

> *"This we know: All things are connected*
> *like the blood which unites one family.*
> *All things are connected.*
> *Whatever befalls the earth*
> *befalls the sons of the earth*
> *Man did not weave the web of life.*
> *He is merely a strand on it.*
> *Whatever he does to the web*
> *He does to himself."*
>
> —Chief Seattle

And so my journeys have ended ...

But do journeys ever really end? Perhaps physically, but they linger in our memory, incubating, until one day we find ourselves seeing with greater clarity: Our prejudice, bigotry, and narrow-mindedness have lessened, our hearts have expanded, and our spirits have lifted.

Many see the world as a great quarry to be mined and a treasure trove to be plundered, and it is. However, for this book, I've selected those places of wonder that most inspired me, because of the extraordinary courage that each has displayed through the centuries. Courage fascinates me. Where does it come from? How does a soldier in Afghanistan manage to grab a live grenade and fling it unthinkingly out of harm's way, thus saving the lives of his teammates? How does a von Staufenberg risk all to eliminate a world menace? How does a sleepy desert village catapult itself out of nowhere to become a quintessential futuristic metropolis—in just a few decades? What propels an Abd al-Rahman, a da Vinci, and a Dante to break radical new ground? What permits a city to withstand an 872-day Nazi siege?

Ernest Hemingway defined courage as "grace under pressure," and Winston Churchill called it "the first of human qualities ... because it is the quality that guarantees all others." Courage is a bedrock. Its presence makes possible the attainment of excellence. I was struck by the almost palpable sense of courage in the places of wonder that I chose to share with you, each a marvel of realization of what human beings have achieved across the centuries.

We are told that our journeys are never really over until we return to share what we have learned with our community. That's probably what the Polish poet, Adam Mickiewicz, had in mind when he observed that "The nectar of life is sweet only when shared with others." As I suggest in my Dubai chapter, when I discuss my Bedouin neighbors, we share a great commonality—even with those who at first seem different. We're all on a common journey. We're all in the process of becoming. And much of life's joy lies in the traveling. The arriving is often anticlimactic. Only in the sharing of what we've experienced—in the taking of stock, in the assessing—can we wisely embark on the next journey. Maybe not in the guise we expected, but as Walt Whitman says in *Song of Myself,* our momentum is "onward and outward ... and nothing collapses."

While living in Florence, I had the pleasure of meeting a remarkable Jesuit priest: Father Tony Lehmann, a popular Dean of Students at the American university that I attended.

Father Tony is remembered and revered by a host of students, colleagues, friends, and acquaintances for his noble heart, but also for a charming little idiosyncrasy: When parting from someone, he never said goodbye. Instead, he said, "To be continued ..."

That struck a chord with me. I want to believe that our journeys will continue—be they international adventures, conversations with special people, or steps in our own immediate evolution—and that such experiences will always come our way. No doubt there will be pauses, digressions, maybe even false starts and dead ends, but the momentum, I believe, is forward and upward.

So in closing, I won't say goodbye, only *To be continued* on another shore.

Acknowledgements

We have long heard the adage "It takes a village to raise a child." It certainly does, but it also takes a village to write a book—an endeavor I could not have undertaken in isolation. First, in all my travels, I required companionship—compatible fellow travelers with whom to share the road. Then I needed teachers--interpreters of what I saw and experienced (guides)—and upon my return home, patient listeners who let me tell my tales. As my recollections began to spill onto paper, I needed advisors--research librarians whom I could never stump; physicians who helped me simplify complicated medical issues; lawyers; foreign language specialists; polishers of prose (editors), an electronic wizard who could make my computer sing and dance; and finally a collection of wise readers—knowing friends, generous souls, who uncomplainingly pored over my manuscript, offering feedback, making suggestions.

Below is a list of those who were available just when I needed them. I shower them with thanks and love:
Ronald H. Clark, Janice C. Condit, Fabrizio Corradini, Anne Catherine de Borman, Fletcher Davis, Ann Derleth, Wick Dufford, Rick Griswold, Phyllis Hatfield, Jo Ann D. Holland, Paul A. Holland, Carole L. Glickfeld, Thomas (Jerry) Greenan, Daniela and Helmut Lieftuchter, John Lucassen, George McDonald, M.D.,

Ursula Meixner [geb v. Korff], Patricia Mesch, Mary Anne Miller, Barbara Pence Moran, Juliana Ochylski, Jim Van Ostrand, M.D., Paul Piecuch, Therese Saliba, Anthony P. Via, S. J., Ph.D.

I also shower my family with thanks and love for their steadfast support.

Author Bio

Rose Marie Curteman is the author of *My Renaisance: A Widow's Healing Pilgrimage to Tuscany.* She was born and raised in Germany, then studied in the United States, earning Bachelor's and Master's degrees in English Literature, a subject she later taught. She makes her home in the Pacific Northwest, but is often in Brussels, Munich, and Tuscany to be with members of her family.

Visit www.rosemariecurteman.com for
additional information, book sales, events and press.